New York University School of Law
Series in Legal History: 1

THE BRIEFS OF THE AMERICAN REVOLUTION

Constitutional Arguments Between Thomas Hutchinson,
Governor of Massachusetts Bay, and
James Bowdoin for the Council and
John Adams for the House of Representatives

Edited by
JOHN PHILLIP REID

Linden Studies in American Constitutional History

New York University Press · New York and London
1981

Library of Congress Cataloging in Publication Data

Massachusetts. Governor (1770–1774 : Hutchinson)
    The briefs of the American Revolution.

    (Series in legal history / New York University School of Law)
    The version of the arguments followed in this text is that of the
pamphlet edition of 1773 sold by the editors of the Boston
Gazette with the title: The speeches of His Excellency Governor
Hutchinson to the general assembly of the Massachusetts-Bay at a
session begun and held on the sixth of January, 1773.
    Bibliography: p.
    Includes index.
    1. Massachusetts—Politics and government—Colonial period,
ca. 1600–1775—Addresses, essays, lectures. I. Bowdoin, James,
1726–1790. II. Adams, John, 1735–1826. III. Reid, John Phillip. IV. Title. V. Series.
J 87.M417 1773a   353.974403°52   81-4079
ISBN 0-8147-7384-2   AACR2

Manufactured in the United States of America

For Professors

GEORGE D. AND LILIAN HERLANDS HORNSTEIN

"Great Teachers"
in New York University

EDITORIAL NOTE

The arguments between Governor Thomas Hutchinson and the Massachusetts council and house of representatives were published several times in 1773: in Boston newspapers, by a legislative journal of Massachusetts Bay, and in a pamphlet sold by the editors of *Boston Gazette,* the colony's most influential whig publication. Although the pamphlet was poorly printed and contained numerous mistakes, it is the version that has been generally followed in preparing the text of this book. It is possible that more eighteenth-century Americans read the debates in this form than in the newspapers. Obvious errors have been corrected, especially with regard to quotations marks which were carelessly placed by the printers of the pamphlet. On the whole, however, the original spelling, punctuation, and capitalization have been retained, even the various spelling of words such as "dependence" and "dependance." The title of the pamphlet is *The Speeches of His Excellency Governor Hutchinson; to the General Assembly of the Massachusetts-Bay. At a Session begun and held on the Sixth of January, 1773. With the Answers of His Majesty's Council and the House of Representatives Respectively. [Publish'd by Order of the House]*.

CONTENTS

INTRODUCTION

"The grand Incendiary of the Province," Thomas Hutchinson remarked in a letter to the commander-in-chief of the British military in North America, was stirring up the population.[1] Hutchinson was the governor of Massachusetts Bay, and he was referring to Samuel Adams. Aroused by reports that "the King had allowed salaries to the Judges of the Superior Court,"[2] a number of the inhabitants of Boston, led by Adams, had petitioned for a town meeting[3] "with an intention," Hutchinson asserted, "to raise a general flame."[4] The meeting had appointed a committee "to state the Rights of the Colonists, and of this Province in particular, as Men, as Christians, and as Subjects."[5] The committee's report, adopted unanimously and published in a pamphlet that was sent to every town in Massachusetts Bay, was

[1] Letter from Governor Thomas Hutchinson to General Thomas Gage, 7 March 1773, Gage, *Papers* [hereinafter cited as Letter].
[2] Ibid.
[3] *Gazette & Post-Boy*, 2 November 1772, at 3, col. 1.
[4] Letter from Governor Thomas Hutchinson to the earl of Dartmouth, 3 November 1772, 5 *Revolution Documents*, at 206.
[5] *Boston Declaration*, at iii.

1

a declaration of principles the governor thought implied "Independence" from Great Britain, and was accompanied by several resolutions "tending to Sedition & mutiny, and some of them expressly denying Parliamentary authority."[6] Samuel Adams and his whig cohorts, Hutchinson wrote, sought "to strike the colonists with the sense of their just claim to independence, and to stimulate them to assert it."[7]

The Boston Declaration, voted by the town meeting on the second of November 1772, is notable in two respects. First, it is one of the very few statements of rights issued by American whigs during the prerevolutionary era that relied on the authority of natural law. Indeed, it may well be considered, along with the preamble of the Declaration of Independence, as the main statement of natural-law arguments issued by a body of colonial whigs. The second notable aspect was the procedure adopted. Not content with merely declaring "the Rights of the Colonists," Boston voters resolved "to Communicate and Publish the same to the several Towns in this Province, and to the World, as the Sense of this Town, with the Infringements and Violations thereof that have been, or from Time to Time may be made; also requesting of each Town a free Communication of their Sentiments on this Subject."[8] It was this feature, the wide dissemination and quest for endorsement, that alarmed Governor Hutchinson, who, ever alert for whig conspiracies, envisioned a plot hatched by Samuel Adams of continental dimensions. "I had," he later recalled, "the fullest evidence of a plan to engage the colonies in a confederacy against the authority of parliament. The towns of this province were to begin; the assemblies to confirm their doings, and to invite the other colonies to join."[9]

The grand incendiary having tried every measure besides to bring the Province into an open declaration of independency,

---

[6] Letter, supra note 1.

[7] Hutchinson, quoted in Cary, *Warren*, at 115.

[8] *Boston Declaration*, at iii.

[9] Letter from Governor Thomas Hutchinson to John Pownall, 14 June 1773, Richard Frothingham, *Life and Times of Joseph Warren* 224 note 1 (1865).

at length projected a plan, 1st, to bring the town of Boston into it, and then into a vote to send their resolves to every other town and district in the Province, with a desire to adopt them, and to appoint committees to correspond with a committee of the town of Boston, and to concert measures for maintaining their principles. The several towns having made these resolves, there would be but little difficulty in bringing their representatives to agree to them in the House; and this being done, the other Assemblies throughout the continent were to be desired by a circular letter to join with the House of Massachusetts Bay.[10]

When about one-third of the 250 or so towns in the colony had met and voted resolutions supporting Boston, Hutchinson decided that he had to take counteraction. "Had I been silent," he explained, "I think scarce any of the rest [of the towns] would have stood out."[11] It was this decision that precipitated the great constitutional debate of 1773.

To publicize the errors of the Boston Declaration and halt its adoption by inland towns, Thomas Hutchinson had a forum that, in ordinary times, was a far more effective platform from which to issue pronouncements that would be more authoritative than mere resolutions of a single town meeting. It was provided by his office: his right as governor to address in joint session the two houses of the colonial legislature known as the great and general court of Massachusetts. Printed in most newspapers, these speeches reached a large audience. Hutchinson knew, however, that to be effective against the Boston Declaration, he had to do more than issue denunciations of Samuel Adams's constitutional heresies that were widely read. He had to convince his readers that Adams was wrong. To accomplish that ob-

[10] Letter from Governor Thomas Hutchinson to Commodore James Gambier, 14 February 1773, Hosmer, *Hutchinson*, at 249 [hereinafter cited as Letter].

[11] Letter, supra note 1. "I knew that these principles were gaining ground in every part of the Province and, if no notice was taken, it would be construed a tacit approbation by the people here, and I had reason to fear it would be deemed a great neglect of my duty to the King." *Ibid.* In an earlier letter, Hutchinson estimated that at least 105 "of the towns, met and passed the same resolves." Letter, supra, note 10.

jective, Hutchinson's first task was to be certain that his purpose was stated clearly. "To do it by slight notice," the governor explained, "would . . . have rather occasioned some sudden rash resolves or votes which having once been passed they [the legislators] would with obstinacy have persisted in; I thought therefore a calm and dispassionate state of the case, if it had not the effect I wished for with the Assembly, yet it would have a good effect with many of the people who I knew were every day through the unwearied pains of the leaders of the opposition made proselytes to these new opinions in government."[12]

It is important to understand precisely what Thomas Hutchinson intended when he began these constitutional debates of the American Revolution. It was not to ask the Massachusetts general court to reject the principles of the Boston Declaration. It was to prove to the legislators and their constituents that those principles "could not be supported," that is to "shew the unwarrantableness of the proceedings by laying before them the true principles of their Constitution in as simple & concise a manner as I could."[13] He was, he repeated a week later, resolved to educate the people of the province, to "show them what their constitution was."[14] For Thomas Hutchinson that constitution was premised on one basic doctrine, the sovereign supremacy of the parliament of Great Britain. The controversy between the colonies and the mother country, he believed, was rooted in the fact that American whigs did not agree with London about the authority of the British legislature. "The source, my lord of all this irregularity," Hutchinson wrote his superior in England, the earl of Dartmouth,

> is a false opinion, broached at the time of the Stamp Act and ever since cultivated until it is become general, that the people of the colonies are subject to no authority but their own

---

[12] Letter from Governor Thomas Hutchinson to the earl of Dartmouth, 7 January 1773, 6 *Revolution Documents*, at 44.

[13] Letter, supra note 1.

[14] Letter, supra note 10, at 250; John R. Galvin, *Three Men of Boston* 245 (1976).

legislatures and that the Acts of the Parliament of Great Britain, which is every day in print termed a foreign state, are not obligatory. All attempts to punish the public asserters of this doctrine and of other seditious and treasonable tenets deduced from it have failed, and whilst this opinion prevails there seems but little room to hope that a grand jury will present[15] or a petty jury convict. Until this opinion prevailed, the people of this province saw the necessity of government and were disposed to support its authority. Could it be eradicated I doubt not the same disposition would again take place.[16]

Governor Hutchinson's method of eradicating the "false opinion" held by his fellow Americans of the supremacy of parliament and the British imperial constitution was not only to educate them by stating correct constitutional principles. He also intended to invite the members of the general court, as an official body, to reply by either agreeing with him or telling him why his explanation of the constitution was wrong.[17] As events turned out, both houses of the legislature did so separately. Hutchinson opened the January, 1773, session of the general court with an address. The council and the house of representatives each answered him. The governor submitted a replication, which again was met with separate rejoinders. Hutchinson came back with a surrejoinder and prorogued the session, giving legislators no opportunity to draft rebutters.

These seven documents, as a unit, constitute the most important constitutional debate of the prerevolutionary era. Indeed, it would be more accurate to call them briefs rather than debates or arguments. They were the briefs of the American Revolution.

At first glance, it may seem loose language to describe speeches in a political forum as judicial briefs. But these

---

[15] That is, indict.

[16] Letter from Governor Thomas Hutchinson to the earl of Dartmouth, 23 October 1772, 5 *Revolution Documents*, at 205.

[17] Letter from Governor Thomas Hutchinson to the earl of Dartmouth, 22 December 1772, 4 *Revolution Documents*, at 223.

seven exchanges between the executive and legislative
branches in Massachusetts Bay were as much legal arguments in a constitutional litigation as are any papers filed
today in a constitutional litigation before the United States
Supreme Court. There was in the eighteenth-century British empire no high tribunal of final adjudication to which
constitutional questions could be brought for argument and
for determination. The British constitution was whatever
could be plausibly argued and forcibly maintained, and the
arguments on both sides of the prerevolutionary controversy were sufficiently plausible as law that both would resort to force to maintain them, the British contending that
the final imperial authority was vested in the king in parliament sitting in Westminster, American whigs denying parliamentary supremacy. Had there, however, been a court to
which this question could have been brought for settlement
binding and acceptable to both sides, it is arguable that the
briefs submitted by opposing attorneys would have more
closely resembled the Massachusetts debates of 1773 than
any other set of prerevolutionary documents.[18] Thomas
Hutchinson stated it was the constitution, and the constitution alone, that was at issue, and he undertook to explain
and defend the imperial constitution as he and the lawyers
of London understood it. The two houses of the general
court answered him in kind. If we find that their arguments
read more like briefs filed by attorneys in a constitutional
litigation than like ordinary legislative messages, we should
not be surprised. They were, in fact, arguing a constitutional case. And they knew they were arguing before the
only tribunal in which that constitutional case legally could
be settled—the court of informed public opinion.

---

[18] For other discussions of the constitutional issues by lawyers of opposing principles see, Adams "Novanglus" against Leonard, "Massachusettenis"; Leigh, *Considerations* against Lee, *Answer;* and Carroll, "First Citizen" against Dulany, "Antilon."

THE ADDRESS
OF THE GOVERNOR

INTRODUCTION

Sending a friend a copy of his address, Thomas Hutchinson apologized "for laboring to prove points so evident." He had to do so, he explained, because "the prejudices people were under made it necessary."[1] That comment sums up part of the difficulties the governor was about to make for himself. He did not appreciate the ideological sincerity of the audience he was addressing. The "points" he labored over may have been "evident" to him but not to most of the people of Massachusetts Bay. The reason was not because they were beset with "prejudices" but because they were persuaded of the constitutional validity of principles differing from those he thought self-evident.

We must not complain. We rather should be grateful that Thomas Hutchinson did not understand that he was speaking to a body of men who never could be persuaded that their constitution made the British parliament supreme in every part of the empire and "in all cases whatsoever." Belief that he yet might convert the unconverted caused

---

[1] Letter from Governor Thomas Hutchinson to Commodore James Gambier, 14 February 1773, Hosmer, *Hutchinson*, at 250.

7

Hutchinson to write what his first biographer called his "most elaborate state papers." "The cause of the Tories in America probably never received a setting-forth more detailed and able."[2] More important, as Daniel Webster later noted, the central constitutional issue, the "question, of the power of parliament over the colonies, was discussed with singular ability."[3]

Governor Hutchinson began the debates by stating his purpose and expectation. It was, he claimed, his duty to speak out against the Boston Declaration, and he invited the general court to answer by delineating his errors, if any there be. His argument was, in fact, directed squarely at the whigs in the legislature, for many issues were raised in anticipation of their contentions. Hutchinson was familiar with their reasoning. That is why he discussed and rejected the emigration theory of rights. It was a favorite of American whigs, as can be seen below in the answer and rejoinder of the house of representatives. The first settlers of the colonies, according to the theory, had departed voluntarily from England to liberate themselves from the power of a religious hierarchy to which they did not subscribe, and from the monarchical and aristocratical political system that governed the mother country. They did not, however, leave behind their rights and privileges as English citizens, but carried them intact into the new world, including the most precious of all English constitutional privileges, the right to be free of taxation and legislation to which they did not consent either in person or through a legal representative.[4]

---

[2] Hosmer, *Hutchinson*, at 252.

[3] Daniel Webster, *A Discourse in Commemoration of the Lives and Services of John Adams and Thomas Jefferson, Delivered in Faneuil Hall, Boston, August 2, 1826*, at 29 footnote (1826).

[4] "They left England as free Adventurers; and, bringing with Them the Obligation of Allegiance to their lawful Sovereign, brought with Them all the Rights of Englishmen." Anonymous, *Considerations Upon the Rights of the Colonists to the Privileges of British Subjects, Introduc'd by a brief Review of the Rise and Progress of English Liberty, and concluded with some Remarks upon our present Alarming Situation* 4 (1766). "But as Englishmen could not be allured to leave their native homes, to labour in uncultivated countries, without a full security for the enjoyment of those liberties, which they had a right to from birth, the fullest assurances and most

Thomas Hutchinson not only rejected the whig version of the emigration theory of rights, he turned it completely on its head. According to his interpretation the first settlers, when they emigrated fron the home islands, did not bring with them all their English rights and privileges. They abandoned some. What they carried to America was a duty of obedience to the imperial government centered in London, including subjection to the supremacy of parliament. "Your ancestors," he wrote on another occasion,

> until their embarkation were subject to Parliamentary authority, and I am willing further to allow that by removing from one part of the empire where they always had been represented in Parliament to another part where they could not be represented, they must be abridged of some of the rights of Englishmen if Parliament still exercised its authority, but you are to remember that this was the voluntary act of your ancestors for their own benefit. They were at full liberty either to stay and enjoy this privilege or to go and be deprived of it, but the Parliament did nothing which your ancestors could urge as a relinquishing of any part of their right. . . . Which, under these circumstances, is more reasonable: that you should lose some part of the rights which you might have enjoyed if you would have remained, or that Parliament should lose all the authority it had over you?[5]

Thomas Hutchinson was two-thirds through his address before he got to what would prove to be the insoluble problem of the American Revolution: how to draw a line be-

---

ample concessions were made to the adventurers, for their encouragement in so arduous an undertaking." Anonymous, *The Late Occurances in North America, and Policy of Great Britain, Considered* 36 (1766).

[5] Hutchinson, "Dialogue," at 373. A variation of the imperial version of the emigration theory was earlier stated by William Knox. "It is one of the fundamental Maxims of our Constitution . . . that no Subject can ever shake off or release himself from that indissoluble Bond of Relation and natural Allegiance he bears to the Laws of his Country, let him be at ever so great Distance from its Seat of Government; so far from it, his Country hath a Right to expect that *he* always entertains those Sentiments of Attachment and Duty as a Subject, which *she*, as his natural Sovereign, hath an unquestionable Right to call forth into Action in any Shape, and whenever the Necessities of her Situation may demand it." [Knox,] *Letter to a Member,* at 10–11.

tween two supreme heads. Although the governor pursued almost to a point of rigidity the conclusion that none logically could be drawn, it must not be thought that the argument made in his opening address was extreme. He was repeating a maxim so obvious to supporters of parliamentary supremacy over the colonies that they thought it need only be stated to be accepted. "There is no possible medium between absolute independence and subjection to the authority of parliament," Daniel Leonard would assert two years later, hoping to win John Adams from his whig ways.[6] It was a concept of political theory universally held by imperialists, from the unknown like Leonard in Massachusetts Bay to the most powerful figures in London government like the earl of Dartmouth, secretary of state for the colonies. "That in every society," Dartmouth wrote Hutchinson less than a month before the debates began,

> there must be somewhere a supreme uncontrollable power, an absolute authority to decide and determine; that wherever such power is found there is of necessity independent sovereignty; that legal subjection to legal government is essential to legal freedom; and that the welfare and happiness of all depend upon the punctual and regular discharge of the duties of each, are principles that no man in his senses can or will deny, which must at one time or other make their way into the minds of men and oblige them to acknowledge . . . that line of law and justice which divides the authority of the ruling power on the one hand from the rights of those who owe obedience to it on the other.[7]

[6] Leonard, "Massachusettenis," at 39. This truism, like many employed by imperialists to make the case for parliamentary supremacy came from Locke. Thus Ambrose Serle quoted Locke: "In a constituted common-wealth, standing upon its own basis, and acting according to its own nature, that is, acting *for the preservation* of the community, there can be but ONE SUPREME POWER, which is the LEGISLATIVE, to which ALL THE REST *are and must be subordinate.*" [Ambrose Serle] *Americans Against Liberty: or, an Essay on the Nature and Principles of True Freedom, Shewing that the Design and conduct of the Americans tend Only to Tyranny and Slavery* 34–35 (3d ed. 1776)

[7] Letter from the earl of Dartmouth to Governor Thomas Hutchinson, 9 December 1772, 5 *Revolution Documents*, at 239–40. "There cannot be a greater absurdity supposed in government, than to admit two legislative authorities in one state, independent of each other." [Ramsay,] *Historical Essay*, at 190.

The constitutional theory was that sovereignty had to be lodged in some person or institution, and neither could be divided nor limited, a legal concept first realized in England when Charles I and parliament competed for a legal supremacy,[8] and one to which many American whigs subscribed almost as strongly as did British imperialists.[9] "It is," William Knox explained, "of the Nature and Essence of all human Governments, that a supreme and absolute Jurisdiction should be lodged somewhere."[10] "That there is an unlimited authority lodged somewhere in every community," another man wrote, "and an unreserved obedience to that authority required of every individual, appears from the nature of government."[11] If a line could be drawn between one authority and a second authority, the first authority would not be unlimited and the obedience owed to it would not be unreserved.[12]

Throughout this, and his later two speeches, Hutchinson's own definitions of law and authority intruded on his argument. He was, from one perspective, very Jeffersonian.

---

[8] *E.g.*, John Cook, *King Charl[e]s His Case: Or, An Appeal to all Rational Men, Concerning His Tryal At the High Court of Justice. Being for the Most part that which was intended to have been delivered at the Bar, if the King had Pleaded to the Charge, and put himself upon a fair Tryal* 21–22 (1649).

[9] "[F]or any people to be supposed under two different legislative authority's at the same time, and for the same parts of government, is (we think) inconsistent with the very nature of government; inconsistent with the governed, and inconsistent with common sense: If therefore we have a right by charter to govern ourselves to any certain Degrees, than on this principle this right must be exclusive in that degree, of all other powers of legislators in the world while these charters continue." Instructions of Ipswich, 21 October 1765, *Boston Post-Boy*, 4 November 1765, at 2, col. 2.

[10] [Knox,] *Letter to a Member*, at 5.

[11] [Phelps,] *Rights of the Colonies*, at 3.

[12] Of course not everyone agreed. A former governor of East Florida told the commons in 1775: "I say it demonstrates a perfect ignorance of the history of civil society to assert (which is the captivating argument used in this House, for breaking down all the barriers of liberty in America) that two independent legislatures cannot exist in the same community, and therefore we are to destroy the whole fabric of those [American] governments which have subsisted for so many years. . . . I say, a free government necessarily involves many clashing jurisdictions, if pushed to the extreme." William Johnstone, "Governor Johnstone's Speech to the House of Commons, November, 1775," in *The American Revolution: The Anglo-American Relation, 1763–1794*, at 85, 88 (Charles R. Ritcheson ed. 1969).

When he spoke of law he meant law in the sense of legislative command, never in the Cokean or Hamiltonian sense of law as a check on arbitrary will and power, whether the prerogative government of a king or the democratic mandates of a representative legislature.[13] From an entirely different perspective Hutchinson was the most tory of Americans. We see this trait when he warns against the dangers of independence. Anarchy will be the result, he insists; the mob in the street will become supreme or the independent states will destroy one another in petty, fraticidal wars.

The toryism of Hutchinson's constitutional thought must not be passed over lightly. It tells us much, not only about Thomas Hutchinson in particular, but about the loyalist persuasion in general. Anarchy was the tory fear. Abuse of government power was the whig fear. In the debates of 1773 Hutchinson warns that without Great Britain's protection the colonies could "become the Prey of one of the other Powers of Europe." To this warning we will see the whig house of representatives reply that "there is more Reason to dread the consequences of absolute uncontrolled supreme power, whether of a Nation or a Monarch, than those of total Independence."

Hutchinson seldom worried about governmental power. Like Edmund Burke and Lord Dartmouth, he believed that although parliament had authority to tax the colonies, it would be more expedient to claim the right but not exercise it.[14] Yet he could not understand why American whigs were so dogmatically obstinate, risking the security of stable government for a theory that one unconstitutional

---

[13] "[I]ts enough for my purpose that the judiciary and executive powers of any government are obliged to carry the laws of it (which are not in their nature immoral) into execution as long as it continues to exist." Hutchinson, "Dialogue," at 397. If laws were immoral, a judge could not rule them invalid. He should not execute them by resigning from the bench.

[14] "I will not scruple to declare . . . [that] the Exercise of that Right, which appears to me to be inherent in and inseparable from the supreme Authority of the State, and which is solemnly declared and confirmed by that Authority, should be suspended and lie Dormant." Letter from the earl of Dartmouth to Speaker Thomas Cushing, 19 June 1773, 24 *Stevens's Facsimiles*, at 2025.

usurpation of governmental power would lead inevitably to more encroachments on their abstract rights.[15] Faced with a choice between whig liberty and tory order, Thomas Hutchinson had no doubt where his duty lay.

> By entering [a] state of government I subject myself to a power constituted over a society of which I become a member. It is immaterial in whom this power is lodged. Such power must be lodged somewhere or there is no government. You [American whig] say, such submission must be intended only in matters that are just. I say, this is no submission at all, for if any man is at liberty to judge what is just and what is unjust and submit or not submit accordingly, he is free, as far as he pleases, from that power to which he professes himself to be a subject; which is a contradiction in terms.[16]

For Thomas Hutchinson these maxims were more than definitions of law and theories of constitutional power. They were self-evident truths. Believing as he did that his explanations and arguments, when subjected to thoughtful, impassionate judgment, were irrefutable, he had reason to hope he could persuade the whigs of their error. As he said at the end of the address, the prerevolutionary controversy was due to disagreements about the imperial constitution, nothing else. If they could be resolved, "we shall put an end to those Irregularities." He was doomed to failure, not because his interpretation of the British constitution was incorrect, but because little in that constitution was as yet self-evident. Even what to him was the most self-evident principle—that no line could be drawn around sovereign power, and that there cannot be *imperium in imperio*[17]—was not as self-evident as he assumed. "Let the terms be defined with precision," a Bostonian wrote to a local newspaper a month after Hutchinson's last speech, "and very few, I apprehend, will be of any other opinion, than that two jurisdictions, in the same state, may each have a *separate supremacy,* no ways

---

[15] Bailyn, "Introduction," to Hutchinson, "Dialogue," at 344.
[16] Hutchinson, "Dialogue," at 391–92.
[17] A state within a state.

inconsistent with each other; or, a single branch of the legislature, the house of Lords, could not, in any instance, be
the *supreme* court of judicature from which there lies no appeal."[18]

Today it is difficult to appreciate the depths of Governor
Hutchinson's confidence that he could terminate the prerevolutionary controversy by clarifying the principles of the
constitution. Our problem is to understand how he, a student of English history knowledgeable about the causes of
the English revolution and the Glorious Revolution, could
have been so obtuse to the substance and merits of the
American whigs' constitutional argument. We can only be
certain that Hutchinson began the debates expecting he
could be persuasive. "At the delivery of the speech," he
wrote a friend the day after giving this address, "the members seemed to be amazed, three-quarters of them having
taken for granted that all that had been done by Parliament
was arbitrary and unconstitutional without having ever been
informed what is their constitution. I flatter myself that it
will be of service."[19] He was correct in at least one respect.
The members of the council and the house of representatives were amazed.

"Governor Hutchinson," John Adams later recalled, "in
the plentitude of his vanity and self-sufficiency, thought he
could convince all America and all Europe that the Parliament of Great Britain had an authority supreme, sovereign,
absolute, and uncontrollable over the Colonies, in all cases
whatsoever. . . . The public stood astonished!"[20]

---

[18] "A Letter from a Gentleman." *Evening-Post,* 5 April 1773, at 1, col. 1.
[19] Letter from Governor Thomas Hutchinson to John Pownall, 7 January 1773,
6 *Revolution Documents,* at 45.
[20] Letter from John Adams to William Tudor, 8 March 1817, 2 Adams, *Works,*
at 311.

THE DOCUMENT

His Excellency the Governor was pleased to open the Assembly with the following Speech to both Houses, viz.
Gentlemen of the Council, and,
Gentlemen of the House of Representatives.

I have nothing in special Command from his Majesty to lay before you at this Time; I have general Instructions to recommend to you, at all Times, such Measures as may tend to promote that Peace and Order upon which your own Happiness and Prosperity as well as his Majesty's Service very much depend. That the Government is at present in a disturbed and disordered State is a Truth too evident to be denied. The Cause of this Disorder appears to me equally evident. I wish I may be able to make it appear so to you, for then I may not doubt that you will agree with me in the proper Measures for the Removal of it. I have pleased myself, for several Years past, with Hopes that the Cause would cease of itself and the Effect with it, but I am disappointed, and I may not any longer, consistent with my Duty to the King and my Regard to the Interest of the Province, delay communicating my Sentiments to you upon a Matter of so great Importance. I shall be explicit and treat the Subject without Reserve. I hope you will receive what I have to say upon it with Candor, and, if you shall not agree in Sentiments with me, I promise you, with Candor likewise, to receive and consider what you may offer in Answer.

When our Predecessors first took Possession of this Plantation or Colony, under a Grant and Charter from the Crown of England, it was their Sense, and it was the Sense of the Kingdom, that they were to remain subject to the supreme Authority of Parliament. This appears from the Charter itself and from other irresistable Evidence. This Supreme Authority has, from Time to Time, been exercised by Parliament and submitted to by the Colony, and hath been, in the most express Terms, acknowledged by the Legislature and, except about the Time of Anarchy and Confusion in England which preceeded the Restoration of King Charles the Second, I have not discovered that it has been called in Question even by private or particular Persons until within seven or eight Years last past.[1] Our Provincial or Local Laws have, in numerous Instances, had Relation to Acts of Parliament made to respect the Plantations in general and this Colony in particular, and in our Executive Courts both Juries and Judges have to all Intents and Purposes, considered such Acts as Part of our Rule of Law. Such a Constitution, in a Plantation, is not peculiar to England but agrees with the Principles of the most celebrated Writers upon the Law of Nations that "when a Nation takes Possession of a distant Country and settles there, that Country, though separated from the principal Establishment or Mother Country, naturally becomes a Part of the State equally with its ancient Possessions"[2]

So much however of the Spirit of Liberty breathes thro' all Parts of the English Constitution, that although from the Nature of Government there must be one supreme Authority over the whole, yet this Constitution will admit of subordinate Powers with legislative and executive Authority, greater or less according to local and other Circumstances. Thus we see a Variety of Corporations formed within the Kingdom with Powers to make and execute such Bylaws as are for their immediate Use and Benefit, the Members of such Corporations still remaining subject to the general Laws of the Kingdom. We see also Governments established in the Plantations which, from their separate and remote Situation, require more general and extensive Powers of Legislation within themselves than those formed within the Kingdom, but subject nevertheless, to all such Laws of the Kingdom as immediately respect them or are designed to extend to them, and accordingly we in this Province have, from the first Settlement of it, been

---

[1] Thus, here at the beginning of his opening address Hutchinson stated the ultimate constitutional issue leading to the Revolutionary war: the supremacy of parliament over the American colonies. By referring to the reign of Charles II, he also introduced the chief constitutional dilemma faced by the imperialists. Parliament and the English constitution in the seventeenth century were quite different institutions from the eighteenth-century parliament and British constitution. Yet for reasons that will be explained, Hutchinson had to base his argument on the assumption that they were similar or, if not the same, that the differences were not legally material.

[2] "When a nation takes possession of a distant country, and settles there, that country, though separated from the principal establishment, or mother-country, naturally becomes a part of the state, equally with its antient possessions." 1 Vattel, *Law of Nations*, at 91 [Book I, Ch. 18, Sec. 210].

left to the Exercise of our legislative and executive Powers, Parliament occasionally though rarely, interposing as in its Wisdom has been judged necessary.

Under this Constitution, for more than One Hundred Years, the Laws both of the supreme and subordinate Authority were in general, duly executed, Offenders against them have been brought to condign Punishment, Peace and Order have been maintained and the People of this Province have experienced as largely the Advantages of Government, as, perhaps, any People upon the Globe, and they have from Time to Time in the most public Manner expressed their Sense of it and, once in every Year, have offered up their united Thanksgivings to God for the Enjoyment of these Privileges and, as often, their united Prayers for the Continuance of them.

At Length the Constitution has been called in Question and the Authority of the Parliament of Great-Britain to make and establish Laws for the Inhabitants of this Province has been, by many, denied. What was, at first, whispered with Caution, was soon after openly asserted in Print and, of late, a Number of Inhabitants in several of the principal Towns in the Province, have assembled together in their respective Towns and, having assumed the Name of legal Town Meetings, have passed Resolves which they have ordered to be placed upon their Town Records, and caused to be printed & published in Pamphlets and News-Papers. I am sorry that it is thus become impossible to conceal what I could wish had never been made public. I will not particularize these Resolves or Votes and shall only observe to you, in general, that some of them deny the supreme Authority of Parliament, and so are repugnant to the Principles of the Constitution, and that others speak of this supreme Authority, of which the King is a constituent Part and to every Act of which his Assent is necessary, in such Terms as have a direct Tendency to alienate the Affections of the People from their Sovereign who has ever been most tender of their Rights, and whose Person, Crown and Dignity we are under every possible Obligation to defend and support. In consequence of these Resolves, Committees of Correspondence are formed, in several of those Towns, to maintain the Principles upon which they are founded.

I know of no Arguments, founded in Reason, which will be sufficient to Support these Principles or to justify the Measures taken in Consequence of them. It has been urged,[3] that the sole Power of making Laws is granted by Charter to a Legislature established in the Province, consisting of the King by his Representative the Governor, the Council and the House of Representatives—that by this Charter there are likewise granted or assured to the Inhabitants of the Province all the Liberties and Immunities of free and natural Subjects, to all Intents Constructions and Purposes whatsoever, as if they had been born within the Realm of England—that it is Part of the Liberties of English Subjects, which has its Foundation in Nature, to be governed by Laws made by their Consent in Person or by their Representative—that the Subjects in this Province are not and cannot be Represented in the Parliament of Great-Britain and, consequently, the Acts of Parliament cannot be binding upon them.

I do not find, Gentlemen, in the Charter such an Expression as *sole* Power or any Words which import it. The General Court has, by Charter, *full* Power to make such Laws as are not repugnant to the Laws of England.[4] A favourable Construction has been put upon this Clause when it has been allowed to intend such Laws of England only as are expres[s]ly declared to respect us. Surely then this is by Charter a Reserve of Power and Authority to Parliament to bind us by such Laws, at least, as are made expressly to refer to us and, consequently, is a Limitation of the Power given to the General Court. Nor can it be contended that by the Liberties of free and natural Subjects is to be understood an Exemption from Acts of Parliament because not represented there, seeing it is provided, by the same Charter, that such Acts shall be in Force; and if they that make the Objection to such Acts will read the Charter with Attention, they must be convinced that this Grant of Liberties and Immunities is nothing more than a Declaration and Assurance on the Part of the Crown that the Place to which their Predecessors were about to remove was and would be considered as Part of the Dominions of the Crown of England, and therefore that the Subjects of the Crown so removing, and those born there or in their Passage thither or in their Passage from thence, would

---

[3] By the town of Boston in the *Boston Declaration*.

[4] The charter of 1691 granted to the general court "full power and Authority from time to time to make ordaine and establish all manner of whol[e]some and reasonable Orders Laws Statutes and Ordinances Directions and Instructions either with penalties or without (soe as the same be not repugnant or contrary to the Lawes of this our Realme of England). . . ." 3 Thorpe, *Charters*, at 1882.

not become Aliens but would throughout all Parts of the English Dominions, wherever they might happen to be, as well within the Colony, retain the Liberties and Immunities of free and natural Subjects, their Removal from or not being born within the Realm notwithstanding. If the Plantations be Part of the Dominions of the Crown, this Clause in the Charter does not confer or reserve any Liberties but what would have been enjoyed without it and what the Inhabitants of every other Colony do enjoy where they are without a Charter. If the Plantations are not the Dominions of the Crown will not all that are born here be considered as born out of the Ligeance of the King of England, and whenever they go into any Part of the Dominions will they not be deemed Aliens to all Intents and Purposes, this Grant in the Charter notwithstanding?

They who claim Exemption from Acts of Parliament by Virtue of their Rights as Englishmen, should consider that it is impossible the Rights of English Subjects should be the same, in every Respect, in all parts of the Dominions.[5] It is one of their Rights as English Subjects to be governed by Laws made by Persons in whose Election they have, from Time to Time, a Voice—They remove from the Kingdom where, perhaps, they were in the full Exercise of this Right to the Plantations where it cannot be exercised or where the Exercise of it would be of no Benefit to them. Does it follow that the Government, by their Removal from one Part of the Dominions to another, loses it's Authority over that Part to which they remove, and that they are freed from the Subjection they were under before; or do they expect that Government should relinquish its Authority because they cannot enjoy this particular Right? Will it not rather be said that, by this their voluntary Removal, they have relinquished for a Time at least, one of the Rights of an English Subject which they might if they pleased have continued to enjoy and may again enjoy whensoever they will return to the Place where it can be exercised?

[5] Hutchinson was not merely stating that political and legal equality between various parts of the British empire was not a constitutional right. He believed that individual rights had to be qualified by the distance people lived from Great Britain, the center of authority. "I doubt whether it is possible to project a system of government in which a colony 3000 miles distant from the parent state shall enjoy all the liberty of the parent state. . . . I wish the good of the colony when I wish to see some further restraint of liberty rather than the connexion with the parent state should be broken." Letter from Thomas Hutchinson to Thomas Whately, 20 January 1769, Hutchinson, *Letters*, at 16.

They who claim Exemption, as Part of their Rights by Nature,[6] should consider that every Restraint which Men are laid under by a State of Government is a Privation of Part of their natural Rights, and of all the different Forms of Government which exist, there can be no two of them in which the Departure from Natural Rights is exactly the same.[7] Even in Case of Representation by Election, do they not give up Part of their natural Rights when they consent to be represented by such Person as shall be chosen by the Majority of the Electors, although their own Voices may be for some other Person? And is it not contrary to their natural Rights to be obliged to submit to a Representative for seven Years, or even one Year, after they are dissatisfied with his Conduct, although they gave their Voices for him when he was elected? This must therefore be considered as an Objection against a State of Government rather than against any particular Form.

If what I have said shall not be sufficient to satisfy such as object to the Supreme Authority of Parliament over the Plantations, there may something further be added to induce them to an Acknowledgment of it which I think will well deserve their Consideration. I know of no Line that can be drawn between the supreme Authority of Parliament and the total Independence of the Colonies: It is impossible there should be two independent Legislatures in one and the same State, for although there may be but one Head, the King, yet the two Legislative Bodies will make two Governments as distinct as the Kingdoms of England and Scotland before the Union. If we might be suffered to be altogether independent of Great-Britain, could we have any Claim to the Protection of that Government of which we are no longer a Part? Without this Protection should we not become the Prey of one or the other Powers of Europe, such as should first seize upon us? Is

[6] It was a favorite technique of Hutchinson's to disparage whig arguments by implying they were based on natural law. In 1776 he even reversed the fable told by more recent historians by claiming that the American rebels had first based their pretentions upon "the natural rights of mankind," and turned to constitutional grievances only after deciding that natural law was not sufficient authority to support their case against the imperial constitution. [Hutchinson,] *Strictures Upon the Declaration,* at 4.

[7] This argument deserves special notice as it illustrates a fact generally ignored by historians. Hutchinson the imperialist, not the colonial whigs, has introduced natural law into the debate. Indeed, as the next two sentences demonstrate, Hutchinson thought the authority of natural law much more persuasive than did the members of the Massachusetts house of representatives.

there any Thing which we have more Reason to dread than Independence? I hope it will never be our Misfortune to know by Experience the Difference between the Liberties of an English Colonist and those of the Spanish, French or Dutch.

If then the Supremacy of Parliament over the whole British Dominions shall no longer be denied, it will follow that the *meer* Exercise of its Authority can be no Matter of Grievance.[8] If it has been or shall be exercised in such Way and Manner as shall appear to be grievous, still this cannot be sufficient Grounds for immediately denying or renouncing the Authority or refusing to submit to it. The Acts and Doings of Authority in the most perfect Form of Government will not always be thought just and equitable by all the Parts of which it consists, but it is the greatest Absurdity to admit the several parts to be at Liberty to obey or disobey according as the Acts of such Authority may be approved or disapproved of by them, for this necessarily works a Dissolution of the Government.[9] The Manner then of obtaining Redress must be by Representations and Endeavours, in such Ways and Forms as the established Rules of the Constitution prescribe or allow in order to make any Matters alledged to be Grievances appear to be really such; but I conceive it is rather the *meer* Exercise of this Authority which is complained of as a Grievance, than any heavy Burdens which have been bro't upon the People by Means of it.

As Contentment and Order were the happy Effects of a Constitution strengthened by universal Assent and Approbation, so Discontent and Disorder are now the deplorable Effects of a Constitution enfeebled by Contest and Opposition. Besides Divisions and Animosities which disturb the Peace of Towns and Families, the Law in some important Cases cannot have its Course, Offenders ordered by Advice of His Majesty's Council to be prosecuted, escape with Impunity and are supported and encouraged to go on offending,—the Authority of Government is bro't into

---

[8] This remarkable statement provides as good an answer as we will ever have as to why Hutchinson started this constitutional debate; he really believed that once people understood the British constitution, the controversy between Great Britain and the colonies would end.

[9] Addressing an eighteenth-century audience, Governor Hutchinson could expect his listeners to know that he was discussing the legal doctrines of passive obedience and non-resistance. For a brief discussion see "Irrelevance of the Declaration," in *Law in the American Revolution and the Revolution in the Law: A Collection of Review Essays on American Legal History* (Hendrik Hartog, editor, 1981).

Contempt, and there are but small Remains of that Subordination which was once very conspicious in this Colony, and which is essential to a well-regulated State.

When the Bands of Government are thus weakened, it certainly behoves those with whom the Powers of Government are intrusted to omit nothing which may tend to strengthen them.

I have disclosed my Sentiments to you without Reserve. Let me intreat you to consider them calmly and not to be too sudden in your Determination. If my Principles of Government are right let us adhere to them. With the same Principles our Ancestors were easy and happy for a long Course of Years together, and I know of no Reason to doubt of your being equally easy & happy. The People, influenced by you will forsake their unconstitutional Principles and desist from their Irregularities which are the Consequence of them, they will be convinced that every Thing which is valuable to them depend upon their Connexion with their Parent State, that this Connexion cannot be continued in any other Way than such as will also continue their Dependance upon the supreme Authority of the British Dominions, and that, notwithstanding this Dependance, they will enjoy as great a Proportion of those Rights to which they have a Claim by Nature or as Englishmen as can be enjoyed by a Plantation or Colony.

If I am wrong in my Principles of Government or in the Inferences which I have drawn from them, I wish to be convinced of my Error. Independence I may not allow myself to think that you can possibly have in Contemplation. If you can conceive of any other constitutional Dependance than what I have mentioned, if you are of Opinion that upon any other Principles our Connexion with the State from which we sprang can be continued, communicate your Sentiments to me with the same Freedom and Unreservedness as I have communicated mine to you.

I have no Desire, Gentlemen, by any Thing I have said to preclude you from seeking Relief, in a constitutional Way, in any Cases in which you have heretofore or may hereafter suppose that you are aggrieved and, although I should not concur with you in Sentiment, I will, notwithstanding, do nothing to lessen the Weight which your Representations may deserve. I have laid before you what I think are the Principles of your Constitution: If you do not agree with me I wish to know your Objections: They may be convincing to me, or I may be able to satisfy you of the Insufficiency of them: In either Case I hope, we shall put an End to those Irregularities, which ever will be the Portion of a Government where the Supreme Authority is controverted, and introduce that Tranquility which seems to have taken Place in most of the Colonies upon the Continent.

The ordinary Business of the Session I will not now particularly point out to you. To the enacting of any new Laws which may be necessary for the more equal and effectual Distribution of Justice, or for giving further Encouragement to our Merchandize, Fishery, and Agriculture, which through the Divine Favour are already in a very flourishing State, or for promoting any Measures which may conduce to the general Good of the Province I will readily give my Assent or Concurrence.

Council Chamber   T. Hutchinson
6 January 1773

THE ANSWER
OF THE COUNCIL

INTRODUCTION

There is no need to summarize what Hutchinson said in his address. A contemporary did that for us when he wrote a Boston newspaper that the governor had failed to prove "that the authority of government is absolute and unlimited—that the British government comprehends within its bounds all the dominions belonging to Great-Britain—that the British legislature is the supreme authority of government—and that there is no other power within that government, which can have a *right* to withstand or controul the supreme authority in any of its proceedings."[1] Another writer expressed pleasure on reading the speech "that a Person of so exalted a Character, had at length appeared to set forth the Grounds and Reasons upon which the Parliament of Great-Britain, doth and hath a Right to, exercise a supreme legislative Authority over us."[2]

Hutchinson, if anything, had been too clear, too explicit. "Our Governor," Samuel Adams said with some regret, "forc[e]d the Assembly to express their Sentiments of so

[1]*Evening-Post*, 5 April 1773, at 1, col. 1
[2][Prescott,] *Calm Consideration*, at 34.

delicate though important a Subject as the supreme Authority of the Parliament of Great Britain over the Colonies."[3]
When the earl of Dartmouth lamented to Thomas Cushing,
speaker of the house of representatives, of "the wild and
extravagant Doctrines that I find contained in their answer
to the Speech of the Governor,"[4] Cushing reminded him of
how emphatically Hutchinson had stated his constitutional
principles and demanded a reply. "The Governor," Cushing pointed out, "was pleased to call on the two Houses, in
such a pressing manner, as amounted to little short of a
Challenge to answer him; The House in their answer to his
Excellency expressed their Grief that they had been driven
into the contemplation of such great & profound Questions,
they discovered their great concern that his Excellency by
his Speech had reduced them to the unhappy alternative
either of appearing by their silence to acquiesce in his Excellency's Sentiments or of thus freely discussing this Point.
It was with the greatest reluctance, to my certain knowledge, they entered into a Controversy which they had heretofore cautiously avoided. It was their duty to God, to their
Country and to their own Consciences that oblidged them
to give such answers as they did."[5]

Should we wonder if Cushing was making excuses that he
hoped would soothe the anger of the cabinet minister in
charge of Britain's colonial policy, it is instructive to consider that earlier Samuel Adams had written virtually the
same to fellow whig John Dickinson. "The Silence of other
Assemblies," he explained, "render[e]d it somewhat difficult
to determine what to say with Propriety. As the Sense of the
Colonies might possibly be drawn from what might be advanced by this Province, you will easily conceive, . . . till the
Sentiments of at least Gentlemen of Eminence out of this
province could be known; at the same time that Silence

[3] Letter from Samuel Adams to John Dickinson, 27 March 1773, 3 Adams, *Writings*, at 13 [hereinafter cited as Letter].
  [4] Letter from the earl of Dartmouth to Speaker Thomas Cushing, 19 June 1773,
24 *Stevens's Facsimiles*, at 2025.
  [5] Letter from Speaker Thomas Cushing to the earl of Dartmouth, 22 August
1773, 24 *Stevens's Facsimiles*, at 2028.

would have been construed as the Acknowledgment of the Governor's Principles and a Submission to the fatal Effects of them."[6] Such became the official whig argument: Thomas Hutchinson had forced the issue, and they had no choice but to respond.[7] Once it was decided that they had to answer, however, they departed from the governor's plan. He had sought a joint statement. The two houses decided to reply separately. In a sense it made little difference. Of the seven papers that constitute the debate, the two of least substance are those contributed by the council. They add very little to the briefs submitted by the house of representatives, and are mostly memorable, not for the principles they state, but for their efforts to avoid the ultimate question.

The answer from the council apparently was written by James Bowdoin, at least Thomas Hutchinson thought it was. Bowdoin was not a lawyer,[8] a fact that surely contributed to his failure to impress the governor. "[B]y his repugnant argument," Hutchinson told General Thomas Gage, "he has exposed himself to contempt."[9] "Can you believe," he asked another friend, "that all those cloudy, inconclusive expressions in the Council's answer come from B? They certainly did, and the contempt with which I have treated them enrages him, but he has compelled me to it."[10]

We may suspect that much of Hutchinson's contempt

[6] Letter, supra note 3, at 13.

[7] "Into such dilemma were they [the two houses] brought by the speech that they were under a necessity of giving such answers to it as they did, or having their conduct construed into an acquiescence with the doctrines contained in it, which would have been an implicit acknowledgment that the Province was in a state of subjection differing very little from slavery. The answers were the effect of necessity, and this necessity occasioned great grief to the two Houses." Letter from the Council and House of Representatives to the earl of Dartmouth, 29 June 1773, 9 (sixth series) *Collections Mass. Hist. Soc'y* 304 (1897).

[8] But he did know enough law to write many of the council's state papers during the prerevolutionary era and, after Independence, to serve as a reviser of Massachusetts statutory law. Gerald W. Gawalt, *The Promise of Power: The Emergence of the Legal Profession in Massachusetts 1760–1840,* at 50–51 (1979).

[9] Letter from Governor Thomas Hutchinson to General Thomas Gage, 7 March 1773, Gage, *Papers.*

[10] Letter from Governor Thomas Hutchinson to Commodore James Gambier, 14 February 1773, Hosmer, *Hutchinson,* at 250.

arose from the fact that he and Bowdoin used some terms differently, and he therefore missed some of Bowdoin's meaning. The council, for example, agreed with Hutchinson that current political unrest was caused by constitutional questions and that, if the constitutional issues were resolved, the controversy would dissipate. It did not, however, agree that the disorders arising from that unrest were unlawful. Hutchinson called them unlawful because they were prohibited by statute and staged in opposition of parliamentary mandates. Bowdoin, by contrast, considered causation a mitigating factor. The disorders were caused by parliament's threats against American rights; they were protests against unconstitutional actions by the British government, and were, therefore, not lawless in the sense Hutchinson used the word. The two men defined "law" differently, Bowdoin in a way that Hutchinson could not intellectually understand.

They also employed different definitions of the word *constitution* or, put another way, they sometimes spoke of two different constitutions. Bowdoin not only rejected Hutchinson's doctrine of parliamentary supremacy, he went so far as to suggest it assumed powers only God could possess. The argument has little persuasion today, and probably did not impress British lawyers of 1773, but nearly 150 years earlier it represented the dominant constitutional theory in England. What Bowdoin was dealing with was the same question that caused Sir Edward Coke, John Hampden, John Pym, and others to oppose Stuart absolutism: the problem of limitations on government. In 1628, when fathering the petition of right, Coke had cited and relied on magna carta and the other statutes that James Bowdoin relied on in his brief. Bowdoin was saying that the constitutional principles that had sent Charles I to his death and toppled James II from his throne were still viable.

Thomas Hutchinson did not recognize the historical roots of Bowdoin's argument. For him the constitution meant parliament's command, and he thought of common law only as private law, not law capable of limiting the arbitrary powers of government. From the perspective of that older constitutional tradition—from the perspective of both seventeenth-century English common lawyers and contemporary American whigs—what Hutchinson's constitution meant was explained by a British writer who noted that "our constitution may be one thing to-day, and another thing to-morrow. It is this or that, or any thing that our legislative authority, for the time being, shall think proper to make it."[11] At one time Englishmen had defended themselves against the royal prerogative by claiming that "law" was above government, that there were "rights" and "privileges" possessed by the people. Under the Hutchinsonian constitution nothing was immutable. Even magna carta no longer held the legal mystique of Cokean liberty. "It must," a Connecticut man noted, "be liable to any alteration, which the parliament see fit to make in it, yea liable to an entire abrogation. And from hence it follows farther, that the English nation have no other liberties but such as lie in the breast of parliament, and can never be known but from day to day, from one session of parliament to another, and may vary as often as the parliament changes, yea as often as the moon."[12]

There were British writers who still clung to the notion that the seventeenth-century constitutional principles that had toppled Charles I and James II from their thrones were still available to limit the power of government and give meaning to individual rights. They were stunned on reading Blackstone's description of the omnipotence of parliament and could not accept the reality of the eighteenth-century constitution.[13] For them the discovery was a trou-

---

[11] [Ramsay,] *Historical Essay*, at 146.

[12] [Ebenezer Devotion,] *The Examiner Examined. A Letter From a Gentleman in Connecticut, To his Friend in London. In Answer to a Letter from a Gentleman in London to his Friend in America: Intitled The Claim of the Colonies to an Exemption from Internal Taxes imposed by Authority of Parliament, examined* 12 (1766).

[13] Willougby Bertie, earl of Abingdon, *Thoughts on the Letter of Edmund Burke, esq; to the sheriffs of Bristol, on the affairs of America* lv–lviii (1777). Just the year before publication of Blackstone's first volume, a legal treatise discussed the royal prerogative much as if the crown were still equal to parliament. [Timothy Brecknock,] *Droit le Roy. Or a Digest of the Rights and Prerogatives of the Imperial Crown of Great-Britain* (1764).

blesome revelation that British liberties were not as secure as once had been thought. For American whigs, by contrast, the same discovery created a constitutional crisis forcing them to question their connection with London. If parliament in which they were not represented was sovereign over "law," they possessed no guarantee against arbitrary government. Benjamin Prescott would sum up the matter after parliament altered the charter of Massachusetts Bay and ordered the port of Boston closed in retaliation for the Tea Party. If the lords and commons, Prescott observed, "have a just and undisputable Right to form, pass into Acts, and carry into Execution, such Bills as these are, they may well be stiled a Supreme Legislature, a Legislature not to be limited, restrained or controuled by the Laws of Men or the Laws of God."[14] For Prescott, as well as for Bowdoin and other American whigs, "law" meant something more than mere legislative command; it meant what it had to Coke, Hampden, and Sidney. That is why, when speaking of "constitutional rights," they meant the seventeenth-century constitution, which, for a time, had made "law"—the law of custom, community consensus, and right reason—supreme over the royal prerogative.

Thomas Hutchinson, because he understood "constitution" to have a different meaning, did not understand the historical legitimacy of the whig argument. Like some writers in Great Britain, he seems to have confused arguments based on seventeenth-century constitutional principles with natural law, or at best treated them as window dressing intended to disguise or make more attractive the weak natural-law grounds on which they thought American whigs stood.[15] As a result Hutchinson did not take as seriously as

[14] [Prescott)] *Calm Consideration,* at 45.

[15] "They [Americans] now lay claim to independency upon national principles: and for this purpose have adopted, as unanswerable, all the arguments of Sidney, Lock[e], and other venerable names, who have, with the utmost propriety, exerted their great abilities in establishing the independency and freedom of the mother country, against the intollerable strides of royal prerogative, under the old constitution." Anonymous, *The Constitutional Right of the Legislature of Great Britain, to Tax the British Colonies in America, Impartially Stated* vii (1768).

he otherwise might have done Bowdoin's citation of old English statutory precedents. "Some of them," Hutchinson would write of American whigs,

> imagine they are as well acquainted with the nature of government, and with the constitution and history of England, as many of their partisans in the kingdom; and they will sometimes laugh at the doctrine of fundamentals from which even Parliament itself can never deviate; and they say it has been often held and denied merely to serve the cause of party, and that it must be so until these unalterable fundamentals shall be ascertained; that the great Patriots in the reign of King Charles the Second, Lord Russell, Hampden, Maynard, &c. whose memories they reverence, declared their opinions, that there were no bounds to the power of Parliament by any fundamentals whatever, and that even the hereditary succession to the Crown might be, as it since has been, altered by the Act of Parliament; whereas they who call themselves Patriots in the present day have held it to be a fundamental, that there can be no taxation without representation, and that Parliament cannot alter it.[16]

If Hutchinson's statement is confusing, it is also unfortunate, for his ideas were similar to those held by his imperial colleagues in London. They knew American discontent was based on constitutional considerations and were prepared to answer them. But the debate was less of a dialogue than either side thought because subtle changes in the meaning of words were too often missed. The failure of communication was never more evident than in Bowdoin's answer for the council and Hutchinson's later replication. When Bowdoin contended that "from the Nature and End of Government, the supreme Authority of every Government is limited, the Supreme Authority of Parliament must be limited," Hutchinson read the words and did not understand them in the sense that Bowdoin hoped. If Hutchinson sensed their familiarity, he quickly dismissed it as a sophism, for obviously Bowdoin was stating not a constitutional

---

[16] [Hutchinson] *Strictures Upon the Declaration*, at 23.

principle but at best a notion of natural law unsupportable by any correct view of British government. In fact, Bowdoin was stating a constitutional principle that Sir Edward Coke utilized to formulate the petition of right and that Charles I cited when he denied the jurisdiction of the Rump Parliament to place him on trial. That London and its agents in America such as Thomas Hutchinson did not recognize its legal stirps helped doom the first British empire.

THE DOCUMENT

On the 25th of January William Brattle, Harrison Gray, James Pitts, James Humphrey, *and* Benjamin Greenleaf, *Esquires, a Committee of his Majesty's Council, waited on the Governor with an Answer to the foregoing* SPEECH, *viz.* [1]

May it please your Excellency,

The Board have considered your Excellency's Speech to both Houses with the Attention due to the Subject of it; and we hope with the Candour you are pleased to recommend to them.

We thank you for the Promise, that "if we shall not agree with you in Sentiments, you will with Candour likewise, receive and consider what we may offer in Answer."

Your Speech informs the two Houses that this Government is at present in a disturbed and disordered State; that the Cause of this Disorder is the unconstitutional Principles adopted by the People in questioning the Supreme Authority of Parliament; and that the proper Measure for removing the Disorder must be the substituting contrary Principles.

Our Opinion of these Heads, as well as on some others proper to be noticed, will be obvious in the Course of the following Observations.

With regard to the present disordered State of the Govern-

---

[1] This committee merely delivered the answer to Hutchinson. The committee appointed to "prepare an answer" had consisted of James Bowdoin, Harrison Gray, James Otis, and Stephen Hall. Sessions for 12 January 1773, *Journal of the House*, at 151.

ment, it can have no Reference to Tumults or Riots: from which this Government is as free as any other whatever. If your Excellency meant only that the Province is discontented, and in a State of Uneasiness, we should intirely agree with you; but you will permit us to say we are not so well agreed in the Cause of it. The Uneasiness, which was a general one throughout the Colonies, began when you inform us the Authority of Parliament was first called in Question, viz. about seven or eight Years ago. Your mentioning that particular Time might have suggested to your Excellency the true Cause of the Origin and Continuance of that Uneasiness.

At that Time the Stamp-Act, then lately made, began to operate: Which with some preceeding and succeeding Acts of Parliament, subjecting the Colonies to Taxes without their Consent, was the original Cause of all the Uneasiness that has happened since; and has occasioned also an Enquiry into the Nature and Extent of the Authority by which they were made. The late Town-Meetings in several Towns are Instances of both. These are mentioned by your Excellency in Proof of a disordered State: But tho' we do not approve some of their Resolves, we think they had a clear Right to instruct their Representatives on any Subject they apprehended to be of sufficient Importance to require it: which necessarily implies a previous Consideration of, and Expression of their Minds on, that Subject: however mistaken they may be concerning it.

When a Community, great or small, think their Rights and Privileges infringed, they will express their Uneasiness in a Variety of Ways: some of which may be highly improper, and criminal. So far as any of an attrocious Nature have taken Place, we would express our Abhorrence of them: and as we have always done hitherto, we shall continue to do, every Thing in our Power to discourage and suppress them. But it is in vain to hope that this can be done effectually so long as the Cause of the Uneasiness, which occasioned them, exists.[2]

Your Excellency will perceive that the Cause you assign is by us supposed to be an Effect derived from the original Cause above-mentioned: the Removal of which will remove its Effects.

---

[2] This was one of the most frequently asserted whig legal arguments: that an action otherwise criminal, such as a riot, might, on a theory of "causation," be justified, and blame imputed to the "cause" rather than the actors.

To obtain this Removal, we agree with you in the Method pointed out in your Speech, where you say, "the Manner of obtaining Redress must be by Representations and Endeavours in such Ways and Forms as the Constitution allows, in order to make any Matters alledged to be Grievances appear to be really such." This Method has been pursued repeatedly. Petitions to Parliament have gone from the Colonies, and from this Colony in particular; but without Success. Some of them, in a former Ministry, were previously shewn to the Minister, who (as we have been informed) advised the Agents to postpone presenting them to the House of Commons 'till the first reading of the Bill they refer'd to: when being presented, a Rule of the House against receiving Petitions on Money Bills was urged for the rejecting of them, and they were rejected accordingly: And other Petitions for want of Formality, or whatever was the Reason, have had the same Fate. This we mention, not by Way of Censure on that honourable House, but in some Measure to account for the Conduct of those Persons, who despairing of Redress in a constitutional Way, have denied the just Authority of Parliament: concerning which we shall now give our own Sentiments, intermixt with Observations on those of your Excellency.

You are pleased to observe, that "when our Predecessors first took Possession of this Colony, under a Grant and Charter from the Crown of England, it was their Sense, and it was the Sense of the Kingdom, that they were to remain Subject to the Supreme Authority of Parliament." And to prove that Subjection the greater Part of your Speech is employed.

In order to a right Conception of this Matter, it is necessary to guard against any improper Idea of the term *Supreme* Authority. In your Idea of it your Excellency seems to include *unlimited* Authority: for you are pleased to say, you "know of no Line that can be drawn between the Supreme Authority of Parliament and the total Independence of the Colonies:" But if no such Line can be drawn a Denial of that Authority in any Instance whatever implies and amounts to a Declaration of total Independence. But if Supreme Authority includes unlimited Authority, the Subjects of it are emphatically Slaves: and equally so whether residing in the Colonies or Great-Britain. And indeed in this Respect all the Nations on Earth, among whom Government exists in any of its Forms, would be alike conditioned: excepting so far as the mere Grace and Favor of their Governors might make a Difference;

"for from the Nature of Government there must be, as your Excellency has observed, one Supreme Authority over the whole."

We cannot think, "that when our Predecessors first took Possession of this Colony it was their Sense, or the Sense of the Kingdom, that they were to remain Subject to the Supreme Authority of Parliament" in this Idea of it. Nor can we find that this appears from the Charter; or that such Authority has ever been exercised by the Parliament, submitted to by the Colony, or acknowledged by the Legislature.

Supreme or unlimited Authority can with Fitness belong only to the Sovereign of the Universe: And that Fitness is derived from the Perfection of his Nature.—To such Authority, directed by infinite Wisdom & infinite Goodness, is due both active and passive Obedience: Which, as it constitutes the Happiness of rational Creatures, should with Chearfulness and from Choice be unlimitedly paid by them.—But with Truth this can be said of no other Authority whatever.[3] If then from the Nature and End of Government, the supreme Authority of every Government is limited, the Supreme Authority of Parliament must be limited; and the Enquiry will be what are the Limits of that Authority with Regard to this Colony?—To fix them with Precision, to determine the exact Lines of Right and Wrong in this Case, as in some others, is difficult; and we have not the Presumption to attempt it. But we humbly hope, that as we are personally and relatively, in our private and public Capacities, for ourselves, for the whole Province, and for all Posterity, so deeply interested in this important Subject, it will not be deemed Arrogance to give some general Sentiments upon it, especially as your Excellency's Speech has made it absolutely necessary.

For this Purpose we shall recur to those Records that contain the main Principles on which the English Constitution is founded; and from them make such Extracts as are pertinent to the Subject.[4]

---

[3] The council is replying to Hutchinson's appeal to the doctrine of "passive obedience" and stating, in orthodox whig terms, the doctrine of legal resistance.

[4] The council cited the "English" not the "British" constitution because the colonial whig case rested on English constitutional principles—in this instance the principle of taxation by consent of representatives. The next four paragraphs provide an example of the pleading dilemma whigs faced when applying these principles, for the council had difficulty wording certain authorities as restraints on government in general, not on the crown alone. Whigs took English constitu-

Magna Charta declares, "that no Aid shall be imposed in the Kingdom, unless by the Common Council of the Kingdom, except to redeem the King's Person, &c." And that "all Cities, Boroughs, Towns and Ports shall have their Liberties and free Customs; and shall have the Common Council of the Kingdom concerning the Assessment of their Aids, except in the Cases aforesaid."

The Statute of the 34th Edward I, de tallagio non concedendo, declares "that no Tallage or Aid should be laid or levied by the King or his Heirs in the Realm, without the Goodwill and Assent of the Arch Bishops, Bishops, Earls, Barons, Knights, Burgesses, and other the Freemen of the Commonalty of this Realm."

A Statute of the 25 Ed.3, enacts "that from thenceforth no Person shall be compelled to make any Loans to the King against his Will, because such Loans were against Reason and the Franchise of the Land."

The Petition of Rights [*sic*] in the 3d of Charles Ist, in which are cited the two foregoing Statutes, declares that by those "Statutes, and other good Laws and Statutes of the Realm, his Majesty's Subjects inherited this Freedom, that they should not be compelled to contribute to any Tax, Tallage, Aid, or other like Charge, not sett by common Consent of Parliament." And the Statute of the I. of William 3d, for declaring the Rights and Liberties of the Subject and set[t]ling the Succession of the Crown declares, "That the levying of Money for or to the Use of the Crown, by Pretence of Prerogative without Grant of Parliament, for longer Time, or in any other Manner than the same is or shall be granted, is illegal."

From these Authorities it appears an essential Part of the English Constitution, that no Tallage or Aid or Tax shall be laid or levied "without the Good Will and Assent of the Freemen of the Commonalty of the Realm."[5] If this could be done without their

---

tional precedents from parliament's struggle to restrain the royal prerogative, and, turning them around, applied them against parliament. Thus, the very constitutional tradition that in Great Britain made parliament supreme, Americans employed to prove parliament was not supreme in colonial affairs.

[5] This sentence summarizes the doctrine that authority to impose taxation is derived from consent of the people taxed. The council, as did all contemporary American whigs, stated it as a principle of English constitutional law. They did not base it on natural law or on the authority of writers such as John Locke. Most British opponents of American constitutional claims, including Thomas Hutchinson, agreed that "consent" was a fundamental rule of the constitution. They dis-

Assent, their Property would be in the highest Degree precarious: or rather they could not with Fitness be said to have any Property at all. At best they would be only the Holders of it for the Use of the Crown; and the Crown be in Fact the real Proprietor. This would be Vassalage in the extreme; from which the generous Nature of Englishmen has been so abhorrent, that they have bled with Freedom in the Defence of this Part of their Constitution, which has preserved them from it: and influenced by the same Generosity, they can never view with Disapprobation any lawful Measures taken by us for the Defence of our Constitution, which intitles us to the same Rights and Privileges with themselves.[6]

These were derived to us from Common Law, which is the Inheritance of all his Majesty's Subjects; have been recognized by Acts of Parliament; and confirmed by the Province Charter, which established its Constitution; and which Charter has been recognized by Act of Parliament also. This Act was made in the second Year of his late Majesty Geo. II for the better Preservation of his Majesty's Woods in America: in which is recited the Clause of the said Charter reserving for the Use of the Royal Navy all Trees suitable for Masts: and on this Charter is grounded the succeeding enacting Clause of the Act. And thus is the Charter implicitly confirmed by Act of Parliament.[7]

From all which it appears, that the Inhabitants of this Colony are clearly intitled to All the Rights and Privileges of free and natural Subjects: which certainly must include that most essential

---

agreed with Americans about the meaning of consent, not its constitutional validity. Hutchinson wrote: "It is an undeniable principle of the English constitution, that *no laws* can oblige the subject except they are agreed on by King, Lords and Commons, in Parliament assembled. The same agreement, & *nothing more,* is necessary in laws for levying taxes." In other words, the doctrine of consent made unconstitutional prerogative taxation by king alone. It did not require that every geographical unit being taxed be represented in parliament. [Hutchinson] "Additions," at 52.

[6] Had the council made this argument not in legal terms (equality within the empire) but historical terms, it would have asserted that Americans claimed the same constitution for which the English had fought against Charles I.

[7] It is not clear why the council argued that parliament had confirmed the charter. As the charter was evidence of the original contract, the purpose may have been to establish a theory of constitutional contract binding parliament or, possibly, of constitutional laches. The result would have been that parliament, as well as the crown, was a party to the original contract. Less likely but also possible might have been a theory of subsequent adoption: that by confirming the charter, parliament adopted the colonial interpretation of the contract.

one, that no Aid or Taxes be levied on them without their own
Consent, signified by their Representatives. But from the Clause
in the Charter relative to the Power granted to the General Court
to make Laws, not repugnant to the Laws of England, your Excellency draws this Inference, that "surely this is by Charter a Reserve of Power and Authority to Parliament to bind us by such
Laws, at least, as are made expressly to refer to us, and consequently is a Limitation of the Power given to the General
Court."—If it be allowed that by that Clause there was a Reserve
of Power to Parliament to bind the Province, it was only by such
laws as were in Being at the Time the Charter was granted: for
by the Charter there is nothing appears to make it refer to any
Parliamentary Laws, that should be afterwards made, and therefore it will not support your Excellency's Inference.

The Grant of Power to the General Court to make Laws runs
thus,—"full Power and Authority, from Time to Time, to make,
ordain and establish all Manner of wholesome and reasonable Orders, Laws, Statutes and Ordinances, Directions and Instructions,
either with Penalties or without (so as the same be not repugnant
or contrary to the Laws of this our Realm of England) as they
shall judge to be for the Good and Welfare of our said Province,"
&c.—We humbly think an Inference very different from your Excellency's, and a very just one too, may be drawn from this Clause,
if Attention be given to the Description of the Orders and Laws
that were to be made.—They were to be wholesome, reasonable
and for the Good and Welfare of the Province, and in order that
they might be so, it is provided that they be "not repugnant or
contrary to the Laws of the Realm," that were then in being: by
which Proviso, all the Liberties and Immunities of free and natural Subjects within the Realm were more effectually secured to
the Inhabitants of the Province agreeable to another Clause in the
Charter, whereby those Liberties and Immunities are expressly
granted to them: and accordingly the Power of the General Court
is so far limited, that they shall not make Orders and Laws to take
away or diminish those Liberties and Immunities.[8]

[8] Bowdoin was saying what Americans had always claimed. During the stamp-act
controversy of 1765 a British publication explained that colonial whigs maintained
that this clause "no more subjected them to the parliament of England, than their
having been laid under the same restraint with regard to the laws of Scotland or
any other country would have subjected them to the parliament of Scotland, or
the supreme authority of any other country." *Annual Register 1765*, reprinted in

This Construction appears to us a just one, and perhaps may appear so to your Excellency if you will please to consider, that by another Part of the Charter effectual Care was taken for preventing the General Assembly passing of Orders and Laws repugnant to, or that in any Way might militate with Acts of Parliament then or since made, or that might be exceptionable in any other Respect whatever: for the Charter reserves to his Majesty the Appointment of the Governor, whose Assent is necessary in the passing of all Orders and Laws: after which they are to be sent to England for the Royal Approbation or Disallowance: by which double Controul effectual Care is taken to prevent the Establishment of any improper Orders or Laws whatever.—Besides, your Excellency is sensible that "Letters Patent must be construed one Part with another, and all the Parts of them together, so as to make the whole harmonize and agree." But your Excellency's Construction of the Paragraph impowering the General Court to make Orders and Laws, does by no means harmonize and agree with the Paragraph granting Liberties and Immunities; and therefore we humbly conceive is not to be admitted: Whereas on the other Construction there is a perfect Harmony and Agreement between them. But supposing your Excellency's Inference just, that by the said former Paragraph (considered by itself) are reserved to Parliament Power and Authority to bind us by Laws made expressly to refer to us. Does it consist with Justice and Equity that it should be considered apart, and urged against the People of this Province with all its Force and without Limitation, and at the same Time the other Paragraph which they thought secured to them the essential Rights and Privileges of free and natural Subjects be rendered of no Validity? If the former Paragraph (in this supposed case) be binding on this People, the latter must be binding on the Crown, which thereby became Guarantee of those Rights and Privileges. Or if must be supposed that one Party is held by a Compact, and the other not: Which Supposition

---

Rebellion in America: A Contemporary British Viewpoint, 1765–1783 (David H. Murdock ed. 1979), at 27. A pamphleteer, also disputing Hutchinson's interpretation of the clause, offered an argument based on a contractual theory. "Was not this, Sir, a mutual compact between England and America . . . ? Though America was by this charter, or agreement, to make no law repugnant to the law of England.— Was not England bound (and did not our ancestors understand it so) by the same honour, to make no laws repugnant to the laws and rights of America?" [Allen,] "To the Governor," at 5.

is against Reason and against Law; and therefore destroys the Foundation of the Inference. However, supposing it well founded, it would not from thence follow, that the Charter intended such Laws as should subject the Inhabitants of the Province to Taxes without their Consent: For (as appears above) it grants to them all the Rights and Liberties of free and natural Subjects: Of which one of the most essential is a Freedom from all Taxes not consented to by themselves.—Nor could the Parties, either Grantor or Grantees, intend such Laws. The Royal Grantor could not, because his Grant contradicts such Intention; and because it is inconsistent with every Idea of Royalty and royal Wisdom, to grant what it does not intend to grant. And it will be readily allowed that the Grantees could not intend such Laws, not only on account of their Inconsistency with the Grant, but because their Acceptance of a Charter, subjecting them to such Laws, would be voluntary Slavery.

Your Excellency next observes, "that it cannot be contended that by the Liberties of free and natural Subjects is to be understood an Exemption from Acts of Parliament, because not represented there, seeing it is provided by the same Charter, that such Acts shall be in Force." If the Observations we have made above, and our Reasoning on them be Just, it will appear that no such Provision is made in the Charter, and therefore that the Deductions and Inferences derived from the Supposition of such Provision, are not well founded. And with Respect to Representation in Parliament, as it is one of the essential Liberties of free and natural Subjects, and properly makes those who enjoy it liable to Parliamentary Acts, so in Reference to the Inhabitants of this Province, who are entitled to all the Liberties of such Subjects, the Impossibility of their being duely represented in Parliament, does clearly exempt them from all such Acts at least, as have been or shall be made by Parliament to Tax them; Representation and Taxation being in our Opinion constitutionally inseperable.

"This Grant of Liberties and Immunities, your Excellency informs us, is nothing more than a Declaration and Assurance on the Part of the Crown, that the Place to which our Predecessors were about to remove, was and would be considered as Part of the Dominions of the Crown, and therefore that the Subjects so removing would not become Aliens, but would, both without and within the Colony retain the Liberties and Immunities of free and natural Subjects."

The Dominion of the Crown over this Country before the Arrival of our Predecessors was meerly ideal. Their Removal hither realized that Dominion, and has made the Country valuable both to the Crown and Nation, without any Cost to either of them from that Time to this. Even in the most distressed State of our Predecessors, when they expected to be destroyed by a general Conspiracy and Incursion of the Indian Natives, they had no Assistance from them. This Grant then of Liberties, which is the only Consideration they received from the Crown for so valuable an Acquisition to it, instead of being violated by military Power, or explained away by nice Inferences and Distinctions, ought in Justice, and with a generous Openness and Freedom, to be acknowledged by every Minister of the Crown, and preserved sacred from every Species of Violation.[9]

"If the Plantation be Part of the Dominion of the Crown this Clause in the Charter (granting Liberties and Immunities) does not, your Excellency observes, confer or reserve any Liberties but what would have been enjoyed without it; and what the Inhabitants of every other Colony do enjoy, where they are without a Charter."—Although the Colonies considered as Part of the Dominions of the Crown are intitled to equal Liberties, the Inhabitants of this Colony think it a Happiness, that those Liberties are confirmed and secured to them by a Charter; whereby the Honour and Faith of the Crown are pledged, that those Liberties shall not be violated. And for Protection in them we humbly look up to his present Majesty, our rightful and lawful Sovereign, as Children to a Father, able and disposed to assist and relieve them; humbly imploring his Majesty, that his Subjects of this Province, ever faithful and loyal, and ever accounted such till the Stamp-Act existed, and who in the late War, and upon all other Occasions, have demonstrated that Faithfulness and Loyalty by their vigorous and unexampled Exertions in his Service, may have their Grievances redressed, and be restored to their just Rights.

[9] Bowdoin was restating one of the major arguments American whigs drew from the original-contract theory: the first settlers, by the very act of establishing the colonies, paid to the king a consideration that executed the contract, making it binding. The point that cannot be emphasized enough is that this is not the social contract of Locke, but a variation of the original contract of English constitutional law. John Phillip Reid, "In Our Contracted Sphere: The Constitutional Contract, the Stamp Act Crisis, and the Coming of the American Revolution," 76 *Columbia Law Review* 21–47 (1976).

Your Excellency next observes "that it is impossible the Rights of English Subjects should be the same in every Respect, in all Parts of the Dominions," and Instances in the Right of being "governed by Laws made by Persons, in whose Election they have a Voice." When "they remove from the Kingdom to the Plantations where it cannot be enjoyed," you ask, "will it not be said, that by this their voluntary Removal, they have relinquished, for a Time at least, one of the Rights of an English Subject, which they might if they pleased, have continued to enjoy, and may again enjoy whensoever they will return to the Place where it can be exercised."

When English Subjects remove from the Kingdom to the Plantations with their Properties, they not only relinquish that Right *de facto,* but it ought to cease in the Kingdom *de jure.* But it does not from thence follow, that they relinquish that Right, in Reference to the Plantation or Colony to which they remove. On the contrary, being become Inhabitants of that Colony, and qualified according to the Laws of it, they can exercise that Right equally with the other Inhabitants of it. And this Right, on like Conditions, will travel with them through all the Colonies, wherein a Legislature, similar to that of the Kingdom, is established. And therefore in this Respect, and we suppose in all other essential Respects, it is not impossible the Rights of English Subjects should be the same in all Parts of the Dominions" under a like Form of Legislature.

This Right of Representation is so essential and indispensible in Regard of all Laws for levying Taxes, that a People under any Form of Government destitute of it, is destitute of Freedom—of that Degree of Freedom, for the Preservation of which, Government was instituted; and without which, Government degenerates to Despotism. It cannot therefore be given up, or taken away, without making a Breach on the essential Rights of Nature.[10]

But your Excellency is pleased to say, that they "who claim Exemption as Part of their Rights by Nature, should consider that

---

[10] For the first time the council relied on natural law for authority, and did so even though representation was a British constitutional right, part of the doctrine of consent. The explanation may be that recent British refutations of American constitutional claims had made representation seem to be a relative rather than absolute principle by modifying it with the doctrine of "virtual representation." See *e.g.,* Anon., *Free and Candid Remarks,* at 13; [Ramsay,] *Historical Essay,* at 194; Anon., *Good Humour,* at 23–24; [Knox,] *Claim of the Colonies,* at 29.

every Restraint which Men are laid under by a State of Government, is a Privation of Part of their natural Rights. Even in Case of Representation by Election, do they not give up a Part of their natural Rights, when they consent to be represented by such Persons as shall be chosen by the Majority of the Electors, although their own Voices may be for some other Person? And is it not contrary to their natural Rights to be obliged to submit to a Representative for seven Years, or even one Year, after they are dissatisfied with his Conduct, although they gave their Voices for him, when he was elected? This must therefore be considered as an Objection against a State of Government rather than against any particular Form."

Your Excellency's Premisses are true, but we do not think your Conclusion follows from them. It is true, that every Restraint of Government is a Privation of natural Right:[11] and the two Cases you have been pleased to mention, may be Instances of that Privation. But as they arise from the Nature of Society and Government; and as Government is necessary to secure other natural Rights infinitely more valuable, they cannot therefore be considered as an Objection either "against a State of Government" or "against any particular Form of it."

Life, Liberty, Property, and the Disposal of that Property with our own Consent, are natural Rights.[12] Will any one put the other in Competition with these, or infer that because those other must be given up in a State of Government, these must be given up also? The Preservation of these Rights is the great End of Government: but is it probable they will be effectually secured by a Government, which the Proprietors of them have no Part in the Direction of, and over which they have no Power or Influence whatever? Hence is deducible, Representation: which being necessary to preserve these invaluable Rights of Nature, is itself, for that Reason, a natural Right, coinciding with, and running into, that great Law of Nature, Self-Preservation.

[11] The council is arguing natural law in answer to Hutchinson who cited natural law as his authority.

[12] Arguments such as this one explain why Hutchinson did not take seriously the council's answer. Bowdoin claimed that "liberty" is a natural right but did not define "liberty." Some of Hutchinson's contemporaries maintained that "liberty" could not exist in society, but only in the state of nature. "Right is Liberty, but *Law*, a Fetter: It is not Liberty, unless we can act as we please. Whatsoever, therefore, is a Law or Restraint to it, must be superimposed upon it." Anonymous, *An Introduction to the Knowledge of the Laws and Constitution of England* 2 (1766).

Thus we have considered the most material Parts of your Speech, and agreeble to your Desire disclosed to you our Sentiments on the Subject of it.

"Independence, as your Excellency rightly judged, we have not in Contemplation." We cannot however adopt "your Principles of Government," or acquiesce in all the Inferences you have drawn from them.

We have the highest Respect for that august Body the Parliament, and do not presume to prescribe the exact Limits of its Authority, yet with the Deference that is due to it, we are humbly of Opinion, that as all human Authority in the Nature of it, is and ought to be limited, it cannot constitutionally extend, for the Reasons we have above suggested, to the levying of Taxes in any Form, on his Majesty's Subjects of this Province.

In such Principles as these "our Predecessors were easy and happy:" and in the due Operation of such, their Descendants the present Inhabitants of this Province have been easy and happy: but they are not so now. Their Uneasiness and Unhappiness are derived from Acts of Parliament, and Regulations of Government, that lately and within a few Years past have been made. And this Uneasiness and Unhappiness, both in the Cause and Effects of them, though your Excellency *seems* and can only seem, to be of a different Opinion, have extended and continue to extend to all the Colonies throughout the Continent.

It would give us the highest Satisfaction to see Happiness and Tranquility restored to the Colonies; and especially to see between Great-Britain and them an Union established on such an equitable Basis as neither of them shall ever wish to destroy. We humbly supplicate the Sovereign Arbiter and Superintendent of human Affairs for these happy Events.

THE ANSWER
OF THE HOUSE

INTRODUCTION

Charles Francis Adams described the answer of the house of representatives as "the most elaborate state-paper of the revolutionary controversy in Massachusetts."[1] It is certainly one that has been republished more frequently than most, but not for reasons of its fame or value. It has been republished partly because its author has not been positively identified. Some historians believe Samuel Adams wrote it, and both it and the house's rejoinder were reprinted by the editor of his writings as his work.[2] Others think it was written by John Adams, and both it and the rejoinder of the house have recently been attributed to him and included among his collected papers.[3] Thomas Hutchinson said the house answer was the joint effort of Northampton lawyer Joseph Hawley and "Adams," but did not indicate which Adams.[4]

---

[1] 2 Adams, *Works,* at 310.

[2] 2 Adams, *Writings,* at 401–26 and 431–54; McIlwain, "Transfer of the Charter," at 60. Some attribute the paper to Samuel Adams and others on the committee appointed to answer Hutchinson, notably Joseph Hawley and John Hancock. Christie & Labaree, *Empire,* at 160.

[3] Robert J. Taylor, "John Adams: Legalist as Revolutionist," 89 *Massachusetts Historical Society Proceedings* 55, 62–63 (1977).

[4] Letter from Governor Thomas Hutchinson to Former Governor Francis Bernard, 23 February 1773, Brown, *Joseph Hawley,* at 125.

The answer of the house most likely was the joint effort of Hawley and the two Adamses. The greater share of credit for its success as a constitutional argument, however, must be accorded to John Adams. The law that is argued is simply beyond the capability of Samuel Adams. He and Joseph Warren had been the principal drafters of the Boston Declaration, and the weaknesses of that document can be attributed to them. It rested on general principles of natural rights which never had a chance of impressing the imperial government in London. Indeed, it may be speculated that a reason Hutchinson was bold enough to start the debate with the assembly was that he was misled by the Boston Declaration into thinking it stated doctrines currently held by the whig leadership and that the assembly would make them the basis of their answer. He then would have triumphed easily. The law argued in the Boston Declaration would have been no match for that of his address.

It is quite possible that Samuel Adams wrote the first draft of the house's answer. If so, it was probably as irrelevant to the constitutional controversy as was the Boston Declaration. Joseph Hawley, a member of the drafting committee, would not accept it. An outstanding trial lawyer who was not a strong student of the imperial constitution, Hawley wanted a more competent expert to work on the project. If we can believe John Adams, it was Hawley who enlisted his help by insisting that the committee invite Adams, even though not a member of the house, to advise them on the law.[5] Unfortunately, Adams wrote his recollections long after the event, when his memory was somewhat questionable.

> When I first met the gentlemen, they had an answer to his Excellency's speech already prepared, neatly and elegantly composed, which I then believed had been written by Samuel Adams, but which I have since had some reason to suspect was drawn at his desire, and with his cooperation, by my friend, Dr. Joseph Warren. It was full of those elementary

[5] 3 *Diary and Autobiography,* at 305.

principles of liberty, equality, and fraternity, which have since
made such a figure in the world; principles which are
founded in nature, and eternal, unchangeable truth, but
which must be well understood and cautiously applied.[6] It is
not safe at all times, and in every case, to apply the *ratio ultima
rerum,*—resort to club law and the force of arms. There was
no answer nor attempt to answer the Governor's legal and
constitutional arguments, such as they were.[7]

"I reasoned, I pleaded, I declaimed with the committee till
I convinced them of the many errors," John Adams later
wrote,[8] and we have reason to believe much of what he says
as so much of the final draft unquestionably bears the
stamp of his constitutional thinking.

> We read the answer, paragraph by paragraph. I suggested
> my doubts, scruples, and difficulties. The committee seemed
> to see and to feel the force of them. The gentlemen conde-
> scended to ask my opinion, what answer would be proper for
> them to report? I modestly suggested to them the expediency
> of leaving out many of those popular and eloquent periods,
> and of discussing the question with the Governor upon prin-
> ciples more especially legal and constitutional. The gentlemen
> very civilly requested me to undertake the task, and I agreed
> to attempt it.
>
> The committee met from evening to evening, and I soon
> made my report. I drew a line over the most eloquent parts
> of the oration they had before them, and introduced those
> legal and historical authorities which appear on the record.[9]

Those "legal and constitutional authorities," Adams would
boast, were "adopted by the committee, and with astonish-
ing unanimity in the House, and . . . convinced the whole
people of North America, and the whole scientific world,

---

[6] "The Draught of a Report was full of very popular Talk and with those dem-
ocratical Principles which have since done so much mischief in this country." Ibid.

[7] Letter from John Adams to William Tutor, 8 March 1817, 2 Adams, *Works,* at
311–12 [hereinafter cited as Letter].

[8] Letter from John Adams to Mercy Warren, 20 July 1807, "Warren Correspondence," at 347 [hereinafter cited as Letter].

[9] Letter, supra note 7, at 313.

that by law and constitution Parliament had no authority over us in any case whatsoever." [10]

Judging by external evidence only, it would seem that John Adams did not have much time to work on the answer. It was delivered to the governor only 20 days after his original address. Moreover, we know Samuel Adams had a hand in writing it, probably helping to rewrite the draft into final form. [11] Finally, the answer is not as well documented as most of John Adams's writings. It relies primarily on easily available works by Thomas Hutchinson, James Otis, and Edward Bancroft. Indeed, much of the argument is lifted directly from a pamphlet Bancroft had published in London four years earlier. Some of Bancroft's evidence was unreliable, a fact Thomas Hutchinson suspected but was apparently unable to prove. Adams and the house could have been badly embarrassed had Hutchinson more time or a more complete library for conducting research.

Bancroft was not a good authority in any event, as his work was anonymous and generally not documented. That John Adams and the drafting committee placed so much reliance on Bancroft's pamphlet may have been due to three factors. First, like the governor, they lacked both the time and the books to write a completely original study. Second, Bancroft seemed reliable. He offered so much evidence to support his legal and constitutional arguments that he conveyed a superficial appearance of thoroughness, implying accuracy. Third, Adams, working in haste, may not have realized the extent to which he depended on the pamphlet, as his reasonings and techniques were quite dissimilar from those Bancroft employed. Bancroft was not a lawyer but a medical student. The contrast between his profes-

[10] Letter, supra note 8, at 347. "How these Papers would appear to me or to others, at this day I know not, having never seen them since their first publication: but they appeared to me, at that time to be correct." 3 *Diary and Autobiography*, at 305.

[11] In a subsequent letter, Samuel Adams refers to a statement in the answer as "*mine,* upon *your* Authority as I thought." Letter from Samuel Adams, 22[?] February 1773, 1 *Papers of John Adams,* at 331.

sional education and Adam's may account for the differences in methodology between his pamphlet and Adams's answer for the house, differences that are revealing about the manner in which the prerevolutionary controversy was argued.

The lawyer, John Adams, was concise, going directly to the point, first stating facts and then drawing conclusions, without much elaboration. The nonlawyer, Edward Bancroft, took greater pains to be certain that his lay readers understood the principles being discussed. An illustration is provided by their discussion of a Virginia statute of 1679, that both claimed Charles II ordered drafted, and sent to Virginia to be enacted *"by the King's most excellent Majesty, by and with the Consent of the General Assembly of Virginia."* John Adams made his point in a single sentence: "If the King had judged that Colony to be a Part of the Realm, he would not, nor could he consistently with Magna Charta, have placed himself at the Head of, and joined with any Legislative Body in making a Law to Tax the People there, other than the Lords and Commons of England." Edward Bancroft took a paragraph to make his point.

> Let me here desire the Reader to observe the Terms in which this Law was expressed, and the Authority by which it was enacted, and then candidly ask himself, whether he imagines that King *Charles,* if he had deemed the Colonies to be mere *English* Corporations . . . would have condescended to be named as a Part of their Legislature: Whether the Terms and Mode of Expression are pertinent to any other than a distinct Sovereign State, and whether, if the King had deemed *Virginia* a Part of the Realm, and subject to Taxation by Parliamentary Authority, he could have joined himself with any other Persons in that Colony in raising Money from the Inhabitants, without violating the fundamental Principles of the *British* Constitution? Would he not, in so doing, have levied Money from the People without Consent of Parliament, contrary to the Great Charter of King *John,* and the Bill and Declaration of Rights?—I am confident, and I insist, that if the Inhabitants of the Colonies are *British* Subjects, and subject to the Authority of a *British* Parliament, the King cannot

lawfully join himself with any other Authority than the Lords and Commons of *Great Britain* in imposing Taxes on them, because *British* Subjects cannot be constitutionally taxed by any other Authority; and that if the late Acts of Parliament, imposing [the Townshend] Duties upon the Importation of *British* Commodities into the Colonies, are just, every other Act for Levying Money, for or to the Use of the Crown in the Colonies, which has received the Assent of the King or his Governors, is unwarrantable; because this double Taxation for the Service of Government is incompatible with the Privileges of a *Briton,* and as a *British American* I protest against it.[12]

The argument was first formulated by Bancroft. He understood its legal significance and stated it well. Adams took from Bancroft's paragraph the basic constitutional conclusion and condensed it into a single sentence. Their method and purpose also tells us something about the role history played in the prerevolutionary controversy. It was used by the nonlawyer Bancroft to persuade as if arguing a political point. It was employed by the lawyer Adams as authority much as he would have quoted a legal maxim, cited a statute, or relied on the report of a court's decision in a litigation.

It is important to understand how and why history was relevant to a discussion of the prerevolutionary imperial constitution. It was not, as often alleged, to seek guidance from past experience[13] or to argue what the constitution ought to be by pretending what it once was.[14] Rather history was argued, not as history, but as law.

[12] Bancroft, *Remarks,* at 69–70.

[13] This is often thought to be the purpose of looking at evidence from classical times. Lawyers knew that like arguments from natural law such evidence could be used by imperialists as easily as by American whigs. For example: "The extension of the right of electing Magistrates to the people at large, was the principal cause of the fall of freedom in Old Rome." [James Macpherson,] *The Rights of Great Britain Asserted against the Claims of America: Being an Answer to the Declaration of the General Congress* 51 (10th ed., 1776).

[14] "The quest of a suitable constitution to give stability to the imperial union was at least a superficial concern of all statesmen who joined in the expanding debate. Perhaps because all were familiar with a British constitution and a common law,

Today in litigation involving the meaning of the United States Constitution, history has a very small role to play—if any role at all. The Constitution is what the federal courts say it is, and history, when useful, is useful for persuading judges that they wish to say such and such. It is seldom useful for proving that the Constitution means such and such. The eighteenth-century imperial British constitution was markedly different. It was rapidly coming to be understood that the British constitution was whatever parliament said it was. That maxim had not yet been generally accepted, and lawyers still discussed constitutional points using a methodology more reminiscent of the seventeenth century than prescient of the nineteenth century. In the earlier century, as well as among American whigs and many British lawyers as late as the 1770s, the meaning of the constitution was formulated by arguing custom, practice, precedent, and institutional functions, not by citing the authority of parliamentary command or judicial reasoning. That is why Edward Bancroft, about to introduce much of the evidence that John Adams would incorporate into the answer of the house, told his readers that to prove that the colonies were not part of the realm of Great Britain he would prove that earlier, during their formative years, they had not been part of the realm of England. To do so, he said, "it will be necessary to review their Political History, the Charters on which they were settled, the Circumstances attending their Settlement, and the Conduct of the King and Parliament towards them since that Era."[15]

The concepts of "constitution" and of "law" were so different in the eighteenth century from what we understand them today, it is necessary to reemphasize a point so that Adams's intention and what he sought to accomplish will be

---

both founded in precedent, all marshaled historical proofs in support of their own particular views of that union. Nearly all sought to expound what the connection *ought to be* by pretending to describe it as it *was*." Anthony Lewis, "Jefferson's *Summary View* as a Chart of Political Union," 5 *William & Mary Quarterly* 34, 37 (1948).

[15] Bancroft, *Remarks,* at 10.

correctly appreciated. During the seventeenth century the constitution had been shaped into a bulwark against royalist absolutism, by claiming that history proved that the common law was ageless, that it must have existed before the king, that the king therefore was subject to "law," and that history proved the supremacy of "law" over the promulgations of institutions that owed their existence to that law. Such history is a perversion of what we today call "history," as it implied a common law which had never changed since time immemorial. John Tyrrell, for example, in 1695 confidently traced English rights and privileges back to the very beginning of the nation, "to our first *English Saxon Kings*," and concluded it was "certain that the Freemen of *England* have always from beyond all times of memory enjoyed the same Fundamental Rights and Privileges (I mean in substance) that they do at this day."[16] Put another way, to claim in terms of constitutional law (though not in terms of non-constitutional common law) "that a precedent exists is to claim that a system of law as old as that precedent is still in force."[17]

To say that the methodology was bad history does not say it was bad law. It was the reverse. It was good law because, between the time of Coke, Hampden, and Pym, and the recognition of sovereignty vested in a supreme parliament, it was the one methodology English lawyers employed to settle constitutional controversies. It was the fact that this methodology was the accepted technique of common lawyers that made history, or rather events proven by history, valid legal authority. To prove what the constitution had once been was to prove what the constitution currently was. That is the reason why John Adams, like Edward Bancroft, turned to history to establish his case. Our proof is not that he did so. Our proof is that Thomas Hutchinson, instead of rejecting Adams's historical evidence out of hand, subjected

---

[16] [James Tyrrell,] *A Brief Enquiry into the Ancient Constitution and Government of England* 10 (1695).

[17] J.G.A. Pocock, *The Ancient Constitution and the Feudal Law: A Study of English Historical Thought in the Seventeenth Century* 47 (1957).

it to the scrutiny of serious legal analysis. He did so in his replication. Practically ignoring the answer of the council, Hutchinson devoted almost all of the replication to arguing the accuracy and relevance of Adams's historical data, and, therefore, the persuasiveness of Adams's law.

THE DOCUMENT

And on the 26th of January *the House of Representatives sent up to his Excellency their Answer, by Mr.* Adams, *Mr.* Hancock, *Mr.* Bacon, *Col.* Bowers, *Major* Hawley *Capt.* Derby, *Mr.* Phillips, *Col.* Thayer, *and Col.* Stockbridge.[1]

May it please your Excellency,

Your Excellency's Speech to the General Assembly at the Opening of this Session, has been read with great Attention in this House.

We fully agree with your Excellency, that our own Happiness as well as his Majesty's Service, very much depends upon Peace and Order; and we shall at all Times take such Measures as are consistent with our Constitution and the Rights of the People to promote and maintain them. That the Government at present is in a very disturbed State is apparent! But we cannot ascribe it to the People's having adopted unconstitutional Principles, which seems to be the Cause assigned for it by your Excellency. It appears to us to have been occasioned rather, by the British House of Commons assuming and exercising a Power inconsistent with the Freedom of the Constitution, to give and grant the Property of the Colonists, and appropriate the same without their Consent.

It is needless for us to enquire what were the Principles that induced the Councils of the Nation to so new and unprecedented a Measure. But when the Parliament by an Act of their own

---

[1] The committee appointed to draft the answer consisted of Thomas Cushing, Samuel Adams, John Hancock, Joseph Hawley, Humphrey Hobson, Ebenezer Thayer, Jedecleah Foster, Samuel Phillips, and Jerathmeel Bowers. Session for 8 January 1773, *Journal of the House,* at 145. The answer, reported out of committee the same day it was "sent up" to the governor, was unanimously adopted by the ninety-seven members present. Session for 26 January 1773, ibid., at 177. The answer was printed in ibid., at 178–90.

expresly declared, that the King, Lords and Commons of the Nation "have, ever had, and of Right ought to have full Power and Authority to make Laws and Statutes of sufficient Force and Validity to bind the Colonies and People of America, Subjects of the Crown of Great-Britain, in all Cases whatever,"[2] and in Consequence hereof another Revenue Act[3] was made, the Minds of the People were filled with Anxiety, and they were justly alarmed with Apprehensions of the total Extinction of their Liberties.

The Result of the free Enquiries of many Persons into the Right of the Parliament to exercise such a Power over the Colonies, seems in your Excellency's Opinion, to be the Cause of what you are pleased to call the present "disturbed State of the Government;" upon which you "may not any longer consistent with your Duty to the King, and your Regard to the Interest of the Province, delay communicating your Sentiments." But that the Principles adopted in Consequence hereof, are unconstitutional, is a Subject of Enquiry. We know of no such Disorders arising therefrom as are mentioned by your Excellency. If Grand Jurors have not on their Oaths found such Offences, as your Excellency with the Advice of his Majesty's Council have *ordered* to be prosecuted, it is to be presumed they have followed the Dictates of good Conscience. *They* are the constitutional Judges of these Matters; and it is not to be supposed, that moved from corrupt Principles, they have suffered Offenders to escape a Prosecution and thus supported and encouraged them to go on offending. If any Part of Authority, shall in an unconstitutional Manner, interpose in any Matter, it will be no wonder if it be brought into Contempt; to the lessening or confounding of that Subordination which is necessary to a well regulated State. Your Excellency's Representation that the Bands of Government are weakened, we humbly conceive to be without good Grounds; though we must own the heavy Burthens unconstitutionally brought upon the People have been and still are universally and very justly complained of as a Grievance.

You are pleased to say, that "when our Predecessors first took Possession of this Plantation or Colony, under a Grant and Charter from the Crown of England, it was their Sense, and it was the Sense of the Kingdom, that they were to remain subject

---

[2] The Declaratory Act, 6 George III, cap. 12.
[3] The Revenue Act of 1766, 6 George III, cap. 52, or the Townshend Duties, 7 George III, cap. 46.

to the Supreme Authority of Parliament;" whereby we understand your Excellency to mean in the Sense of the Declaratory Act of Parliament aforementioned, in all Cases whatever. And indeed it is difficult, if possible, to draw a Line of Distinction between the universal Authority of Parliament over the Colonies, and no Authority at all. It is therefore necessary for us to enquire how it appears, for your Excellency has not shown it to us, that when or at the Time that our Predecessors took Possession of this Plantation or Colony, under a Grant and Charter from the Crown of England, it was *their Sense,* and the Sense of the *Kingdom,* that they were to remain subject to the Supreme Authority of Parliament. In making this Enquiry, we shall, according to your Excellency's Recommendation, treat the Subject with Calmness and Candor, and also with a due Regard to Truth.

Previous to a direct Consideration of the Charter granted to this Province or Colony, and the better to elucidate the true Sense and Meaning of it, we would take a View of the State of the English North American Continent at the Time when and after Possession was first taken of any Part of it, by the Europeans. It was then possessed by Heathen and Barbarous People, who had nevertheless all that Right to the Soil and Sovereignty in and over the Lands they possessed, which God had originally given to Man. Whether their being Heathen, inferred any Right or Authority to Christian Princes, a Right which had long been assumed by the Pope, to dispose of their Lands to others, we will leave to your Excellency or any one of Understanding and impartial Judgment to consider. It is certain they had in no other Sense forfeited them to any Power in Europe. Should the Doctrine be admitted that Discovery of Lands owned and possessed by Pagan People, gives to any Christian Prince a Right and Title to the Dominion and Property, still it is vested in the Crown alone. It was an Acquisition of Foreign Territory, not annexed to the Realm of England and therefore at the absolute Disposal of the Crown.[4] For we take it to be a settled Point, that the King has a constitutional Prerogative

---

[4] Another New England whig explained the same legal concept more clearly when he wrote: "REALM signifies kingdom; and kingdom signifies the country or countries, that are subject to one sovereign prince. And should a school boy be asked, whether America, which is three thousand miles distant, was within the kingdom of Great-Britain, both being subject to one prince, he must answer that it was not; but that it was within the kingdom of the King of Great-Britain and America." [Mather,] *America's Appeal,* at 30.

to dispose of and alienate any Part of his Territories not annexed to the Realm.[5] In the Exercise of this Prerogative, Queen Elizabeth granted the first American Charter; and claiming a Right by Virtue of Discovery, then supposed to be valid, to the Lands which are now possessed by the Colony of Virginia, she conveyed to Sir Walter Rawleigh, the Property, Dominion and Sovereignty thereof, to be held of the Crown by Homage, and a certain Render, without any Reservation to herself of any Share in the Legislative and Executive Authority. After the Attainder of Sir Walter, King James the First created two Virginia Companies, to be governed each by Laws transmitted to them by his Majesty, and not by the Parliament, with Power to establish and cause to be made a Coin to pass current among them; and vested with all Liberties, Franchises and Immunities within any of his other Dominions, to all Intents and Purposes, as if they had been abiding, and born *within the Realm.* A Declaration similar to this is contained in the first Charter of this Colony, and in those of other American Colonies; which shows that the Colonies were not in-

---

[5] Quoting this sentence a government pamphleteer would later comment: "I leave it to my readers to determine whether the following proposition is not more agreeable to the fundamental principles of the British constitution: 'I take it to be a settled point, that the king, as king, has no constitutional prerogative to acquire any territories, that are not annexed to the Realm'. Who would have expected to have found such very zealous advocates for royal prerogative among the puritanical inhabitants of New England." [Gray,] *Right of the Legislature,* at 36. This observation stated a principle constitutionally correct at the time. The rule stated by the house was carelessly phrased for it seems to be claiming a prerogative right belonging to the crown in 1773 when, to make his case, Adams needed only to have proven belonged to the first two Stuarts, the kings at the time the first colonies had been settled. It was immaterial to Adams's case whether kings in the eighteenth century still possessed the same right. That Adams put the argument in the present tense is indicative of how even good eighteenth-century lawyers did not take into consideration the fact that, over periods of time, the constitution was altered in both substance and theory. The argument Adams sought to make was important however. Its legal implications had been explained in 1769 as follows: "From the earliest times, down to the present, the disposition of foreign territory belonging to Great-Britain, has always been vested in the Executive. It is a power which the Restoration and the Revolution have left unshaken. . . . If then the Crown, at the time when it granted the charters, could have ceded the territory of America to a foreign power, could it not have fixed the terms, on which its present and future inhabitants should continue the subjects of Great Britain? Where it could have relinquished *all* the authority possessed by Great Britain, certainly it could relinquish a *part* of that authority. Where it could make a total *alienation,* to enemies even, surely it could make a *modified grant,* to subjects." Anon., *Case of Great Britain,* at 2.

tended or considered to be within the Realm of England, though within the Allegiance of the English Crown. After this, another Charter was granted by the same King James, to the Treasurer and Company of Virginia, vesting them with full Power and Authority, to make, ordain and establish all Manner of Orders, Laws, Directions, Instructions, Forms and Ceremonies of Government and Magistracy, fit and necessary, and the same to abrogate, &c. without any Reservation for securing their Subjection to the Parliament and future Laws of England. A third Charter was afterwards granted by the same King to the Treasurer and Company of Virginia, vesting them with Power and Authority to make Laws, with an Addition of this Clause, "so always that the same be not contrary to the Laws and Statutes of this our Realm of England." The same Clause was afterwards copied into the Charter of this and other Colonies, with certain Variations, such as that these Laws should be "consonant to Reason," "not repugnant to the Laws of England," "as nearly as conveniently may be to the Laws, Statutes and Rights of England," &c. These Modes of Expression convey the same Meaning, and serve to show an Intention that the Laws of the Colonies should be as much as possible, conformant in the Spirit of them to the Principles and fundamental Laws of the English Constitution, its Rights and Statutes then in Being; and by no Means to bind the Colonies to a Subjection to the Supreme Authority of the English Parliament.[6] And that this is the true Intention, we think it further evident from this Consideration, that no Acts of any Colony Legislative, are ever brought into Parliament for Inspection there, though the Laws made in some of them, like the Acts of the British Parliament are laid before the King for his Assent or Disallowance.

We have brought the first American Charters into View, and the State of the Country when they were granted, to show that the Right of disposing of the Lands was in the Opinion of those Times vested solely in the Crown—that the several Charters conveyed to the Grantees, who should settle upon the Territories therein granted, all the Powers necessary to constitute them free and distinct States—and that the fundamental Laws of the English Constitution should be the certain and established Rule of Legis-

---

[6] This sentence indicates how extensively Adams borrowed from Edward Bancroft's pamphlet. Bancroft, also using the term "Mode of Expression," concluded "that the Clause was not inserted to bind the Colonies to obey Acts of Parliament, but only to limit and modulate their Government and Laws upon Principles conformable to the Constitution of *England*." [Bancroft,] *Remarks,* at 21.

lation, to which the Laws to be made in the several Colonies were to be as nearly as conveniently might be, conformable or similar; which was the true Intent and Import of the Words, "not repugnant to the Laws of England," "consonant to Reason," and other variant Expressions in the different Charters. And we would add, that the King in some of the Charters reserves the Right to judge of the Consonance and Similarity of their Laws with the English Constitution to himself, and not to the Parliament; and in Consequence thereof to affirm, or within a limited Time, disallow them.

These Charters, as well as that afterwards granted to Lord Baltimore, and other Charters, are repugnant to the Idea of Parliamentary Authority: And to suppose a Parliamentary Authority over the Colonies under such Charters, would necessarily induce that Solecism in Politics *Imperium in Imperio.* And the King's repeatedly exercising the Prerogative of disposing of the American Territory by such Charters, together with the Silence of the Nation thereupon, is an Evidence that it was an acknowledged Prerogative.

But further to show the Sense of the English Crown and Nation that the American Colonists and our Predecessors in particular, when they first took Possession of this Country by a Grant and Charter from the Crown, did not remain subject to the Supreme Authority of Parliament, we beg Leave to observe; that when a Bill was offered by the two Houses of Parliament to King Charles the First, granting to the Subjects of England the free Liberty of Fishing on the Coast of America, he refused his Royal Assent, declaring as a Reason, that "the Colonies were *without the Realm and Jurisdiction of Parliament."* [7]

---

[7] Adams obtained this quotation from Bancroft who wrote: *"Charles* the First, by whom the *Plymouth, Massachusetts,* and *Maryland* Charters were soon after granted" refused the royal assent, saying "that the Colonies were without the Realm and Jurisdiction of Parliament, and that the Privy Council would take order in Matters relating to them, though a little after, when the *Maryland* Charter was granted, he reserved to the subjects of *England* the same right of Fishing upon the Coast of that Province, which was intended to be secured by the Bill that was denied the Royal Assent; which abundantly proves that the King did not refuse the Bill for any secret Reasons, but only because he thought it might afford a Precedent for an unwarranted extension of Parliamentary Jurisdiction." [Bancroft,] *Remarks,* at 24. Bancroft may have fabricated that precedent. Like Adams, he cited no authority so we cannot be certain. What is evident is that Charles I vetoed no bill on free fishing as none was enacted by Parliament. Lounsbury, *British Fishery,* at 51; 1 *Papers of John Adams,* at 330 n 2.

In like Manner, his Predecessor James the First, had before declared upon a similar Occasion, that America *was not annexed to the Realm,* and it was not fitting that Parliament should make Laws for those Countries. This Reason was, not secretly, but openly declared in Parliament. If then the Colonies were not annexed to the Realm, at the Time when their Charters were granted, they never could be afterwards, without their own special Consent, which has never since been had, or even asked.[8] If they are not now annexed to the Realm, they are not a Part of the Kingdom, and consequently not subject to the Legislative Authority of the Kingdom. For no Country, by the Common Law was subject to the Laws or to the Parliament, but the Realm of England.[9]

We would if your Excellency pleases, subjoin an Instance of Conduct in King Charles the Second, singular indeed, but important to our Purpose; who, in 1679, framed an Act for a permanent Revenue for the Support of Virginia, and sent it there by

[8] "[I]f the Crown (as is evident) had a Right to constitute distinct States in *America;* and if the Colonies, according to the Royal Intention and Construction, were so constituted, and if they were peopled and planted on this Principle and Condition, it will follow, as a necessary Consequence, that no Power on Earth could afterwards unite them to the Realm of *England,* or subject them to the Authority of its Parliament, without their own special Consent, given in the same formal and solemn Manner as was done by the Kingdom of *Scotland,* at its union with England." [Bancroft,] *Remarks,* at 25.

[9] In his replication Hutchinson singled out this statement and claimed that it was not law and could not be sustained by authority leading John Adams, in the house's rejoinder, to cite a published judicial opinion. It should be understood why the house of representatives, when making this argument, relied on the common law rather than on the constitution as its authority. Again the influence of Edward Bancroft is apparent. After pointing out that the first statute of parliament ever extended to the colonies was the navigation act of 12 Charles II, Bancroft had argued:

It is however to be lamented, that the then Parliament had not thought proper to discover, for the Information of Posterity, the Source from whence it derived the Right of making Laws, not only for all Countries under his Majesty's Dominion in *Asia, Africa,* and *America,* but for all Countries which hereafter may belong to, or be in the Possession of "his Heirs and Successors," as it must doubtless have been new and hitherto undiscovered; since however extensive the King's Prerogative may be over his foreign Subjects, the *English* Constitution has made no Provision for this Species of National, External Legislation, the Power of Parliament being originally confined to the Limits of the Realm, and the Nation collectively, of which it was the Representing and Legislative Assembly. How far the Parliament . . . departed from the primitive Spirit of our Constitution, let others judge.

[Bancroft,] *Remarks,* at 53.

Lord Colpepper [*sic*], the Governor of that Colony; which was afterwards passed into a Law, and *"Enacted by the King's most excellent Majesty, by and with the Consent of the General Assembly of Virginia."* [10] If the King had judged that Colony to be a Part of the Realm, he would not, nor could he consistently with Magna Charta, have placed himself at the Head of, and joined with any Legislative Body in making a Law to Tax the People there, other than the Lords and Commons of England.

Having taken a View of the several Charters of the first Colony in America, if we look into the old Charter of this Colony,[11] we shall find it be grounded on the same Principle: That the Right of disposing the Territory granted therein was vested in the Crown, as being that Christian Sovereign who first discovered it, when in the Possession of Heathen; and that it was considered as being not within the Realm, but only within the Fee and Seignory of the King. As therefore it was without the Realm of England, must not the King, if he had designed that the Parliament should have had any Authority over it, have made a special Reservation for that Purpose? which was not done.

Your Excellency says, it appears from the Charter itself, to have been the Sense of our Predecessors who first took Possession of this Plantation or Colony, that they were to remain subject to the Authority of Parliament. You have not been pleased to point out to us how this appears from the Charter, unless it be in the Observation you make on the above-mentioned Clause, viz. "That a favourable Construction has been put upon this Clause, when it has been allowed to intend such Laws of England only as are expresly made to respect us," which you say "is by Charter a Reserve of Power and Authority to Parliament to bind us by such Laws at least as are made expresly to refer to us, and consequently is a Limitation of the Power given to the General Court." But we would still recur to the Charter itself, and ask your Excellency, How this appears from thence to have been the Sense of our Predecessors? Is any Reservation of Power and Authority to Parliament thus to bind us, expressed or implied in the Charter? It is evident, that King Charles the first, the very Prince who granted it, as well as his Predecessor, had no such Idea of the Supreme Authority of Parliament over the Colony from their Declarations

---

[10] "An Act for raising a publique revenue for the better support of the government of this his majesties colony" (June 1680), *Hening Statutes,* at 466–69.

[11] That is, the first or original Massachusetts charter.

before recited. Your Excellency will then allow us further to ask, by what Authority in Reason or Equity the Parliament can enforce a Construction so *unfabourable* to us. *Quod ab initio injustum est, nullum potest habere juris effectum,* said *Grotius.* Which with Submission to your Excellency may be rendered thus, *Whatever is originally in its Nature wrong, can never be sanctified or made right by Repetition and Use.*

In Solemn Agreements subsequent Restrictions ought never to be allowed. The celebrated Author whom your Excellency has quoted, tells us that "neither the one or the other of the interested or contracting Powers hath a right to interpret at Pleasure."[12] This we mention to show, even upon a Supposition that the Parliament had been a Party to the Contract, the Invalidity of any of its subsequent Acts, to explain any Clause in the Charter; more especially to restrict or make void any Clause granted therein to the General Court. An Agreement ought to be interpreted "in such a Manner as that it may have *its Effect:*" But if your Excellency's Interpretation of this Clause is just, "that it is a Reserve of Power and Authority to Parliament to bind us by such Laws as are made expresly to refer to us," it is not only "a Limitation of the Power given to the General Court" to Legislate, but it may whenever the Parliament shall think fit, render it of *no Effect;* for it puts it in the Power of Parliament to bind us by as many Laws as they please, and even to restrain us from making any Laws at all. If your Excellency's Assertions in this and the next succeeding Part of your Speech were well grounded, the Conclusion would be undeniable, that the Charter even in this Clause, "does not confer or reserve any Liberties" worth enjoying, "but what would have been enjoyed without it;" saving that within any of his Majesty's Dominions we are to be considered barely as *not Aliens.* You are pleased to say, it cannot "be contended that by the Liberties of free and natural Subjects" (which are expresly granted in the Charter to all Intents, Purposes, and Constructions whatever) "is to understood an Exemption from Acts of Parliament because not represented there; seeing it is provided by the same Charter that such Acts shall be in Force." If, says an eminent Lawyer, "the King grants to the Town of D. the same Liberties which London has, this shall

[12] "The third general maxim, or principle, on the subject of interpretation is: *That neither the one nor the other of the interested, or contracting powers, has a right to interpret the act, or treaty, at his pleasure.*" 1 Vattel, *Law of Nations,* at 216 [Book II, Ch. 17, Sec. 265].

be intended the like Liberties." A Grant of the Liberties of free
and natural Subjects is equivalent to a Grant of the same Liberties.
And the King in the first Charter to this Colony expressly grants
that it "shall be construed, reputed and adjudged in all Cases most
favourably on the Behalf and for the Benefit and Behoof of the
said Governor and Company and their Successors—any Matter,
Cause or Thing whatsoever to the contrary notwithstanding." [13] It
is one of the Liberties of free and natural Subjects, born and abiding within the Realm, to be governed as your Excellency observes,
"by Laws made by Persons in whose Elections they from Time to
Time have a Voice." This is an essential Right. For nothing is
more evident, than that any People who are subject to the unlimited Power of another, must be in a State of abject Slavery. It was
easily and plainly foreseen that the Right of Representation in the
English Parliament could not be exercised by the People of this
Colony.[14] It would be impracticable, if consistent with the English
Constitution. And for this Reason, that this Colony might have
and enjoy all the Liberties and Immunities of free and natural
Subjects within the Realm, as stipulated in the Charter, it was necessary, and a Legislative was accordingly constituted within the
Colony; one Branch of which consists of Representatives chosen
by the People, to make all Laws, Statutes, Ordinances, &c. for the
well ordering and governing the same, not repugnant to the Laws
of England, or, as nearly as conveniently might be, agreeable to
the fundamental Laws of the English Constitution. We are therefore still at a Loss to conceive where your Excellency finds it *"provided* in the same Charter, that such Acts," viz. Acts of Parliament
made expressly to refer to us, "shall be in Force" in this Province.
There is nothing to this Purpose expressed in the Charter, or in
our Opinion even implied in it. And surely it would be very absurd, that a Charter, which is evidently formed upon a Supposition and Intention, that a Colony is and should be considered as
not within the Realm; and declared by the very Prince who
granted it, to be not within the Jurisdiction of Parliament, should
yet *provide,* that the Laws which the same Parliament should make
expresly to refer to that Colony, should be in Force therein. Your

[13] This sentence is not a direct quotation but a paraphase of a long, rather involved grant of immunity in the charter of 1629. See 3 Thorpe, *Charters,* at
1859–60.
   [14] This argument, a favorite of Samuel Adams's, may be evidence that he helped
to write the answer.

Excellency is pleased to ask, "Does it follow that the Government by their (our Ancestors) Removal from one Part of the Dominions to another, loses its Authority over that Part to which they remove: And that they were freed from the Subjection they were under before?" We answer, if that Part of the King's Dominions to which they removed was not then a Part of the Realm, and was never annexed to it, the Parliament lost no Authority over it, having never had such Authority; and the Emigrants were consequently freed from the Subjection they were under before their Removal: The Power and Authority of Parliament being constitutionally confined within the Limits of the Realm and the Nation collectively, of which alone it is the Representing and Legislative Assembly. Your Excellency further asks, "Will it not rather be said, that by this their voluntary Removal, they have relinquished for a Time at least, one of the Rights of an English Subject, which they might if they pleased have continued to enjoy, and may again enjoy, whenever they return to the Place where it can be exercised?" To which we answer; They never did relinquish the Right to be governed by Laws made by Persons in whose Election they had a Voice. The King stipulated with them that they should have and enjoy all the Liberties of free and natural Subjects born within the Realm, to all Intents, Purposes and Constructions whatsoever; that is, that they should be as free as those who were to abide within the Realm: Consequently he stipulated with them that they should enjoy and exercise this most essential Right, which discriminates Freemen from Vassals, uninterruptedly in its full Sense and Meaning; and they did and ought still to exercise it, without the Necessity of returning, for the Sake of exercising it, to the Nation or State of England.

We cannot help observing, that your Excellency's Manner of Reasoning on this Point, seems to us to render the most valuable Clauses in our Charter unintelligible: As if Persons going from the Realm of England to inhabit in America, should hold and exercise there a certain Right of English Subjects: but in Order to exercise it in such Manner as to be of any Benefit to them, they must *not inhabit* there, but return to the Place where alone it can be exercised. By such Construction, the Words of the Charter can have no Sense or Meaning. We forbear remarking upon the Absurdity of a Grant to Persons born within the Realm, of the same Liberties which would have belonged to them if they had been born within the Realm.

Your Excellency is disposed to compare this Government to the Variety of Corporations formed within the Kingdom, with Power to make and execute By-Laws, &c. And because they remain Subject to the Supreme Authority of Parliament, to infer that this Colony is also subject to the same Authority: This Reasoning appears to us not just. The Members of those Corporations are Resiant [*sic*] within the Kingdom; and Residence subjects them to the Authority of Parliament, in which they are also represented: Whereas the People of this Colony are not Resident within the Realm. The Charter was granted with the express Purpose to induce them to reside without the Realm; consequently they are not represented in Parliament there. But we would ask your Excellency; Are any of the Corporations formed within the Kingdom, vested with the Power of erecting other subordinate Corporations? Of enacting and determining what Crimes shall be Capital? And constituting Courts of Common Law with all their Officers, for the hearing, trying and punishing capital Offenders with Death? These and many other Powers vested in this Government, plainly show that it is to be considered as a Corporation in no other Light, than as every State is a Corporation. Besides, Appeals from the Courts of Law here, are not brought before the House of Lords; which shows that the Peers of the Realm are not the Peers of America: But all such Appeals are brought before the King in Council, which is a further Evidence that we are not within the Realm.

We conceive enough has been said to convince your Excellency, that when our Predecessors first took Possession of this Plantation or Colony by a Grant and Charter from the Crown of England, it *was not* and never had been the Sense of the Kingdom, that they were to remain subject to the Supreme Authority of Parliament. We will now with your Excellency's Leave, enquire what *was* the Sense of our Ancestors of this very important Matter.

And as your Excellency has been pleased to tell us, you have not discovered that the Supreme Authority of Parliament has been called in Question even by private and particular Persons, until within seven or eight Years past; except about the Time of the Anarchy and Confusion in England, which preceeded the Restoration of King Charles the Second; we beg leave to remind your Excellency of some Parts of your own History of Massachusetts-Bay. Therein we are informed of the Sentiments of "Persons of Influence" after the Restoration, from which the Historian tells us, some parts of their Conduct, that is of the General Assembly, "may be pretty well accounted for." [15] By the History it appears to have been the Opinion of those Persons of Influence, "that the Subjects of any Prince or State had a natural Right to remove to any other State or to another Quarter of the World, unless the State was weakened or exposed by such Remove; and even in that Case, if they were deprived of the Right of all Mankind, Liberty of Conscience, it would justify a Separation, and *upon their Removal their Subjection determined and ceased.*" [16] That "the Country to which they had removed, was claimed and possessed by independent Princes, whose Right to the Lordship and Sovereignty thereof had been acknowledged by the Kings of England," [17] an Instance of which is quoted in the Margin; [18] "That they themselves had actually purchased for valuable Consideration, not only the Soil, but the Dominion, the Lordship and Sovereignty of those Princes;" without which Purchase, "in the Sight of God and Men, they had no Right or Title to what they possessed." [19] That they had received a Charter of Incorporation from the King, from whence arose a new Kind of Subjection, namely, "a voluntary, civil Subjection," and by this Compact "they were *to be governed by Laws made by themselves.*" [20] Thus it appears to have been the Sentiments

[15] The reference is to a paragraph in Hutchinson's *History* discussing the commissioners sent to Massachusetts by Charles II. Their authority was disputed and Hutchinson claimed that sufficient documents existed to understand the grounds upon which the colonists disputed it. 1 Hutchinson, *Massachusetts Bay,* at 215–16.

[16] Ibid., at 216.

[17] Ibid.

[18] That is, quoted in a footnote. In that footnote Hutchinson told of a prosecution in England of a "buccaneer" for piracy against the Spaniard in South America. The defendant was "acquitted because he had a commission from the Indian Princes of Darien." *Ibid.*

[19] Ibid.

[20] Ibid., at 216–17. The quotations, although reasonably accurate, are taken out of context. Hutchinson's next two sentences (not quoted) would have denied the conclusion Adams wanted the reader to draw. Hutchinson said, "But however pleasing these principles were in speculation, or whatever foundation they may have in nature, yet they could not continue to practise upon them, nor would they bear the test when adopted by English subjects. In a short time they were content fully to comply with the oath of allegiance without qualifying it, and to give up other points, which they had before insisted upon; and their posterity, who claim by birthright as well as charter the peculiar priviliges of Englishmen, and who enjoy the protection, are very sensible that they likewise owe the allegiance of English subjects, which by a general rule of law is not considered as local, but perpetual and unalienable." Ibid., at 217.

of *private* Persons, though Persons by whose Sentiments the public Conduct was influenced, that their Removal was a justifiable Separation from the Mother State, upon which their Subjection to that State determined and ceased. The Supreme Authority of Parliament, if it had then ever been asserted, must surely have been called in Question, by Men who had advanced such principles as these.

The first Act of Parliament made expressly to refer to the Colonies, was after the Restoration. In the Reign of King Charles the Second, several such Acts passed. And the same History informs us there was a Difficulty in conforming to them; and the Reason of this Difficulty is explained in a Letter of the General Assembly to their Agent, quoted in the following Words, "They apprehended them to be an Invasion of the Rights Liberties and Properties of the Subjects of his Majesty in the Colony, *they not being represented in Parliament,* and according to the usual Sayings of the Learned in the Law, the Laws of England were bounded within the four Seas, *and did not reach America:* However as his Majesty had signified his Pleasure that those Acts should be observed in the Massachusetts, they had made Provision by a Law of the Colony that they should be strictly attended." [21] Which Provision by a Law of their own would have been superfluous, if they had admitted the Supreme Authority of Parliament. In short, by the same History it appears that those Acts of Parliament as such were disregarded; and the following Reason is given for it; "It seems to have been a *general* Opinion that Acts of Parliament had no other Force, than what they derived from Acts made by the General Court to establish and confirm them." [22]

But still further to show the Sense of our Ancestors respecting this Matter, we beg leave to recite some Parts of a Narrative presented to the Lords of Privy Council by Edward Randolph, in the Year 1676, which we find in your Excellency's Collection of Papers lately published. Therein it is declared to be the Sense of the Colony "that no Law is in Force or Esteem there, but such as are made by the General Court; and therefore it is accounted a Breach of their Privileges, and a Betraying of the Liberties of their Common-wealth, to urge the Observation of the Laws of England." [23] And further, "That no Oath shall be urged or re-

[21] Ibid., at 272.

[22] 2 Hutchinson, *Massachusetts Bay,* at 3.

[23] "Copy of a Paper endorsed M.E.R's. Narrative Sept. 20th and Octo. 12th 1676." [Hutchinson,] *Collection of Papers,* at 482.

quired to be taken by any Person, but such Oath as the General Court hath considered, allowed and required."[24] And further, "there is no notice taken of the Act of Navigation, Plantation or any other Laws made in England for the Regulation of Trade."[25] "That the Government would make the World believe they are a free State, and do act in all Matters accordingly."[26] Again, "These Magistrates ever reserve to themselves a Power to alter, evade and disannul any Law or Command, not agreeing with their Humour or the absolute Authority of their Government, acknowledging no Superior."[27] And further, "He the (Governor) freely declared to me, that the Laws made by your Majesty and your Parliament, obligeth them in nothing, but what consists with the Interests of that Colony, that the Legislative Power and Authority is and abides in them *solely*."[28] And in the same Mr. Randolph's Letter to the Bishop of London, July 14, 1682, he says, "This *Independency* in Government, claimed and daily practised."[29] And your Excellency being *then* sensible that this was the Sense of our Ancestors, in a Marginal Note in the same Collection of Papers, observes, that "this, viz. the Provision made for observing the Acts of Trade, is very extraordinary, for this Provision was an Act of the Colony declaring the Acts of Trade shall be in Force there."[30] Although Mr. Randolph was very unfriendly to the Colony, yet as his Declaration are concurrent with those recited from your Excellency's History, we think they may be admitted for the Purpose for which they are now brought.[31]

[24] Ibid., at 483.
[25] Ibid., at 496.
[26] Ibid.
[27] Ibid., at 499.
[28] The house "doctored" this quotation, attributing to the governor a stronger statement than actually made. According to the document Hutchinson published, Randolph said that he was told "that the legislative power is and abides in them solely to act and make lawes by virtue of a charter from your Majesties royall father, . . . and that your Majestie ought not to retrench their liberties, but may enlarge them if your Majestie please." "A short narrative . . . ," ibid., at 506. By inserting the word "authority" for additional emphasis, and by ending the sentence at the word "solely," the house made it appear that the governor, when talking to Randolph, claimed "legislative Power and Authority" as an inherent right, and not merely as a grant by the charter.
[29] "Copy of a letter from Mr. Edward Randolph to the Lord Bishop of London," 14 July 1682, ibid., at 539.
[30] Ibid., at 521 note.
[31] The "Purpose" to which the house refers should not be misunderstood. It was different than the purpose intended above when evidence was offered of the in-

Thus we see, from your Excellency's History and Publications, the Sense our Ancestors had of the Jurisdiction of Parliament under the first Charter. Very different from that which your Excellency *in your Speech* apprehends it to have been.

It appears by Mr. Neal's History of New-England, that the Agents who had been employed by the Colony to transacts [*sic*] it[s] Affairs in England at the Time when the present Charter was granted, among other Reasons gave the following for their Acceptance of it, viz. "The General Court has with the King's Approbation as much Power in New-England, as the King and Parliament have in England; they have all English Privileges, and can be touched by *no Law,* and by no Tax but of their own making."[32] This is the earliest Testimony that can be given of the Sense our Predecessors had of the Supreme Authority of Parliament under the present Charter. And it plainly shows that they, who having been freely conversant with those who framed the Charter, must have well understood the Design and Meaning of it, supposed that the Terms in our Charter "full Power and Authority," intended and were considered as a *sole* and exclusive Power, and that there was no "Reserve in the Charter to the Authority of Parliament, to bind the Colony" by any Acts whatever.

Soon after the Arrival of the Charter, viz in 1692, your Excellency's History informs us, "the first Act" of this Legislative was a Sort of Magna Charta, asserting and setting forth their general Privileges, and this Clause was among the rest, "No Aid, Tax, Tallage, Assessment, Custom, Loan, Benevolence, or Imposition whatever, shall be laid, assess'd, impos'd or levied on any of their Majesty's Subjects, or their Estates, on any Pretence whatever, but by the Act and Consent of the Governor, Council and Representatives of the People assembled in General Court."[33] And though this Act was disallowed, it serves to show the Sense which the General Assembly contemporary with the granting the Charter had of

---

tent and actions of James I and Charles I. Then the technique had been to employ history as a means of proving an authoritative precedent. The purpose of the historical recital in the last several paragraphs was not to prove a legal precedent but (by demonstrating intent and understanding) to prove legal custom and usage.

[32] The history book cited by the house quoted the agents as claiming all English "Liberties" not "all English Privileges." Neal, *History of New England,* at 479; 2 Neal, *History* (2d ed.), at 106. Bancroft, who cited no authority quoted the agents as claiming "all *English* Privileges and Liberties." [Bancroft,] *Remarks,* at 72.

[33] 2 Hutchinson, *Massachusetts Bay,* at 48.

their sole and exclusive Right to Legislate for the Colony. The History says, "the other Parts of the Act were copied from Magna Charta;" [34] by which we may conclude that the Assembly then construed the Words "not repugnant to the laws," to mean, comformable to the fundamental Principles of the English Constitution. And it is observable that the Lords of Privy Council, so lately as in the Reign of Queen Anne, when several Laws enacted by the General Assembly, were laid before her Majesty for her Allowance, interpreted the Words in this Charter, "not repugnant to the Laws of England," by the Words "as nearly as conveniently may be agreeable to the Laws and Statutes of England." And her Majesty was pleased to disallow those Acts, not because they were repugnant to any Law or Statute of England, made expresly to refer to the Colony; but because divers Persons, by Virtue thereof, were punished without being tried by their Peers in the ordinary "Courts of Law," and "by the ordinary Rules and known Methods of Justice;" contrary to the express Terms of Magna Charta, which was a Statute in Force at the Time of granting the Charter, and declaratory of the Rights and Liberties of the Subjects within the Realm. [35]

You are pleased to say, that "our Provincial or Local Laws have in numerous Instances had Relation to Acts of Parliament made to respect the Plantations and this Colony in particular." The Authority of the Legislature, says the same Author who is quoted by your Excellency, "does not extend so far as the Fundamentals of the Constitution." "They ought to consider the Fundamental Laws as sacred, if the Nation has not in very express Terms, given them the Power to change them. For the Constitution of the State ought to be fixed: And since that was first established by the Nation, which afterwards trusted certain Persons with the Legislative Power, the fundamental Laws are excepted from their Commission." [36] Now the Fundamentals of the Constitution of this Province are stipulated in the Charter; the Reasoning therefore in this

[34] Ibid., at 48–49. In his history Hutchinson did not speculate as to why the bill was disallowed.

[35] Hutchinson did not discuss these vetoes in his *History*.

[36] 1 Vattel, *Law of Nations*, at 18 [Book I, Ch. 3, Sec. 34] This statement was written by a Swiss lawyer, and if applicable at all, was applicable to the seventeenth-century English constitution, not the eighteenth-century British constitution. It may have been inserted here because it was familiar, having been given wide circulation in one of the most famous whig pamphlets, [Otis,] *Rights*, at 72.

Case holds equally good. Much less then ought any Acts or Doings of the General Assembly, however numerous, to neither of which your Excellency has pointed us, which barely relate to Acts of Parliament made to respect the Plantations in general, or this Colony in particular, to be taken as an Acknowledgment of this People, or even of the Assembly, which inadvertently passed those Acts, that we are subject to the Supreme Authority of Parliament. And with still less Reason are the Decisions in the Executive Courts[37] to determine this Point. If they have adopted that "as Part of the Rule of Law," which in Fact is not, it must be imputed to Inattention or Error in Judgment, and cannot justly be urged as an Alteration or Restriction of the Legislative Authority of the Province.

Before we leave this Part of your Excellency's Speech, we would observe, that the great Design of our Ancestors, in leaving the Kingdom of England, was to be freed from a Subjection to its spiritual Laws and Courts, and to worship God according to the Dictates of their Consciences. Your Excellency in your History observes, that their Design was "to obtain for themselves and their Posterity the Liberty of worshipping God in such manner as appeared to them most agreeable to the sacred Scriptures."[38] And the General Court themselves declared in 1651, that "seeing just Cause to fear the Persecution of the then Bishop, and High Commission for not conforming to the Ceremonies of those under their Power, they thought it their safest Course, to get to this Outside of the World, out of their View and *beyond their Reach.*"[39] But if it had been their Sense, that they were still to be subject to the Supreme Authority of Parliament, they must have known that their Design might and probably would be frustrated; that the Parliament, especially considering the Temper of those Times,

[37] The reference is to what today are called "courts." During the eighteenth century the two houses of the legislature were courts of law, hence the term "executive" distinguished other courts from "legislative" courts. "[H]owever we may refine and define, there is no more than two powers in any government, viz. the power to make laws, and the power to execute them; for the judicial power is only a branch of the executive." Anon., *Four Letters,* at 21.

[38] 1 Hutchinson, *Massachusetts Bay,* at 352.

[39] "Copy of a petition to the Parliament in 1651," ibid., at 428. The meaning of this sentence was garbled by careless copying. The original version said that they feared "the persecution of the then bishops and high commission, for not conforming to the ceremonies then pressed upon the consciences of those under their power. . . ."

might make what ecclesiastical Laws they pleased, expressly to refer to them, and place them in the same Circumstances with Respect to religious Matters, to be relieved from which was the Design of their Removal. And we would add, that if your
Excellency's Construction of the Clause in our present Charter is
just, another Clause therein, which provides for Liberty of Conscience of all Christians except Papists, may be rendered void by
an Act of Parliament made to refer to us, requiring a Conformity
to the Rites and Mode of Worship in the Church of England, or
any other.[40]

Thus we have endeavoured to shew the Sense of the People of
this Colony under both Charters; and if there have been in any
late Instances a Submission to Acts of Parliament,[41] it has been in
our Opinion, rather from Inconsideration or a Reluctance at the
Idea of contending with the Parent State, than from a Conviction
or Acknowledgement of the Supreme Legislative Authority of
Parliament.

Your Excellency tells us, "you know of no Line that can be
drawn between the Supreme Authority of Parliament and the total Independence of the Colonies." If there be no such Line, the
Consequence is, either that the Colonies are the Vassals of the
Parliament, or, that they are totally Independent. As it cannot be
supposed to have been the Intention of the Parties in the Compact, that we should be reduced to a State of Vassallage, the Conclusion is, that it was their Sense, that we were thus Independent.
"It is Impossible, your Excellency says, that there should be two
independent Legislatures in one and the same State." May we not
then further conclude, that it was their Sense that the Colonies
were by their Charters made distinct States from the Mother
Country? Your Excellency adds, "For although there may be but
one Head, the King, yet the two Legislative Bodies will make two
Governments as distinct as the Kingdoms of England and Scotland before the Union." Very true, may it please your Excellency;
and if they interfere not with each other, what hinders but that
being united in one Head and common Sovereign, they may live
happily in that Connection, and mutually support and protect

[40] The constitutional authority giving to this argument validity was the "original
contract."

[41] The acts referred to are the sugar act of 1764 (4 George III, cap. 15) and the
retention of the tax on imported tea following repeal of the other Townshend
duties.

each other?[42] Notwithstanding all the Terrors which your Excellency has pictured to us as the Effects of a total Independence, there is more Reason to dread the Consequences of absolute uncontrouled Supreme Power, whether of a Nation or a Monarch, than those of a total Independence. It would be a Misfortune "to know by Experience, the Difference between the Liberties of an English Colonist and those of the Spanish, French and Dutch:" And since the British Parliament has passed an Act which is executed even with Rigour, though not voluntarily submitted to, for raising a Revenue, and appropriating the same without the Consent of the People who pay it, and have claimed a Power making such Laws as they please to order and govern us, your Excellency will excuse us in asking, whether you do not think we already experience too much of such a Difference, and have not Reason to fear we shall soon be reduced to a worse Situation than that of the Colonies of France, Spain or Holland?

If your Excellency expects to have the Line of Distinction between the Supreme Authority of Parliament, and the total Independence of the Colonies drawn by us, we would say it would be an arduous Undertaking; and of very great Importance to all the other Colonies: And therefore, could we conceive of such a Line, we should be unwilling to propose it, without their Consent in Congress.[43]

[42] From the beginning of the prerevolutionary controversy until 1776, American whig lawyers insisted that the colonies were connected with the mother country only through the crown. That is why the Declaration of Independence indicted George III despite the fact that the "crimes" for which he was indicted had been committed not by him but by parliament. In a sense, American whigs, by asking the king to revive and exercise the veto in imperial affairs, were among Britain's last constitutional royalists. Their conception of imperial unity must not be associated, as it often is, with the later British commonwealth of nations. Again the Americans faced a pleading dilemma. They sought to preserve their liberty by strengthening the crown, the very institution that in contemporary constitutional theory threatened liberty in Great Britain.

[43] That the house (for political reasons) would not *explicitly* state the constitutional conclusion does not mean that Adams, *et al.*, were pretending they had not stated it *implicitly*. As the speaker of the house explained to the earl of Dartmouth, the opinion of the house members "upon this delicate and Important Subject may, by some be Inferred from the principles they have advanced, yet they cautiously avoided *in Express Terms* to deny the Supream Authority of Parliament, nay they declined upon a matter so interesting & important so much as to attempt to draw a line of distinction between the Supream Authority of Parliament and the total independency of the Colonies." Letter from Speaker Thomas Cushing to the earl of Dartmouth, 22 August 1773, 24 *Stevens's Facsimiles*, at 2028.

To conclude, These are great and profound Questions. It is the Grief of this House, that by the ill Policy of a late injudicious Administration, America has been driven into the Contemplation of them. And we cannot but express our Concern, that your Excellency by your Speech has reduced us to the unhappy Alternative, either of appearing by our Silence to acquiesce in your Excellency's Sentiments, or of thus freely discussing this Point.

After all that we have said, we would be far from being understood to have in the least abated that just Sense of Allegiance which we owe to the King of Great-Britain, our rightful Sovereign: And should the People of this Province be left to the free and full Exercise of all the Liberties and Immunities granted to them by Charter, there would be no Danger of an Independance on the Crown. Our Charters reserve great Power to the Crown in its Representative, fully sufficient to balance, analagous to the English Constitution, all the Liberties and Privileges granted to the People. All this your Excellency knows full well—And whoever considers the Power and Influence, in all their Branches, reserved by our Charter to the Crown, will be far from thinking that the Commons of this Province are too Independent.

INTRODUCTION

A few days after receiving the answer of the house, and more than two weeks before completing his reply, Thomas Hutchinson told Lord Dartmouth, secretary of state for the colonies, that he would have to continue the debate. A replication to both the council and house was necessary, he said, to "show them from undeniable authority what was their constitution at the beginning and what it still continues to be and what must be the fatal consequences of departing from it."[1]

There can be no doubt that the answers shocked the governor. He had not expected the house of representatives to take so strong a stand. "I have," he wrote a friend while drafting the replication, "always avoided the point of the supremacy of Parliament,—I have taken it for granted that it was not to be disputed."[2] Perhaps he had expected that they would back away and that is why he had forced the issue. As previously noted, American whig lawyers were

[1] Letter from Governor Thomas Hutchinson to the earl of Dartmouth, 1 February 1773, 6 *Revolution Documents*, at 80.

[2] Letter from Governor Thomas Hutchinson to Commodore James Gambier, 14 February 1773, Hosmer, *Hutchinson*, at 249.

75

compelled to face the question only three times during the
prerevolutionary crisis. First they did so when parliament
suspended the assembly of New York[3] and the assembly
avoided a confrontation, second when James Bowdoin,
Samuel Adams, and their colleagues had to decide whether
to answer Hutchinson directly or find some means to evade
the implications of his constitutional theory, and third when
Parliament exercised its supremacy, passed the coercive acts,[4]
and the colonies rebelled.

Whether we conclude that the house in its answer met the
issue or evaded it successfully, the central legal and historical fact is that everyone involved understood that Hutchinson had done more than state the ultimate constitutional
question. He had stated what was, in his terms, the constitution itself. Certainly that is what Arthur Lee understood.
The Virginia whig was in London when he read the debates
and wrote Samuel Adams of his delight. At last American
constitutional boundaries were so well marked they should
not again be confused.

> At first it was a tender point to question the authority of par-
> liament over us *in any case* whatsoever; time and you have
> proved that their right is equally questionable *in all cases*
> whatsoever. It was certainly a great stroke, and has succeeded
> most happily. It will remain an authentic record to vouch in
> opposition to their declaratory act,[5] whenever the great and
> ultimate question is seriously brought forward. It stands un-
> controverted. . . . This proud usurping parliament must
> humble itself before us, and acknowledge the liberties of
> America and England to have the same sacred foundation.[6]

It was attitudes such as Arthur Lee's as much as the arguments of James Bowdoin and John Adams that Hutch-

---

[3] 7 George III, cap. 59.

[4] The Boston Port Act, 14 George III, cap. 19; The Massachusetts Government
Act, 14 George III, cap. 45; The Administration of Justice Act, 14 George III,
cap. 39; The Quartering Act, 14 George III, cap. 54.

[5] 6 George III, cap. 12.

[6] Letter from Arthur Lee to Samuel Adams, 13 October 1773, 1 Lee, *Arthur Lee*,
at 236–37.

inson had to overcome in his replication. He could not do so directly, for there was little he could add to his earlier argument that no line could be drawn around sovereignty. He had stated it as an absolute principle that could not be made more absolute. He chose, therefore, to analyze the historical evidence marshaled by John Adams to prove parliament was not sovereign over the colonies. In the process, Hutchinson paid scant attention to the answer of the council. He claimed Bowdoin's arguments were so erroneous they could be dismissed with contempt, but it may be wondered if he failed to appreciate just how much substance the council's answer contained. Bowdoin, it will be recalled, relied on certain fundamentals that he associated with magna carta, the petition of right, and other milestones of English constitutional development. Hutchinson considered them irrelevant authority. "Although," he explained,

> all these statutes were enacted to limit the authority of one branch [of parliament] only, the king, without including the other branches of the legislative power [lords and commons], and make no mention of any limits to the united authority of all the branches; yet they [the council] endeavour to improve them to their purpose, by changing the idea of limits to the degree of the supreme power, for that of the local limits by which the exercise of this supreme power is to be bounded.[7]

That was why Hutchinson ignored the principal argument of the council: because he considered it only from the anachronistic perspective of the eighteenth-century constitution of parliamentary sovereignty. Writing of himself in the third person, he explained that the council's "pretense to unalterable fundamentals, by *compact,* or stipulation between them and the crown of England, he treated as a meer chimera, seeing not only grants made by the crown, but the crown itself, upon the principles of the English constitution, were liable to be controuled & regulated by the Supreme legislative power."[8]

[7] 3 Hutchinson, *Massachusetts Bay,* at 267–68.
[8] Hutchinson, "Additions," at 58.

It was the answer of the house that impressed Hutchinson and he concentrated his main attention on what he thought its chief argument, the distinction between the crown and realm of England. Had he reflected on the matter, Hutchinson may have been pleased that John Adams had been the leading brief writer for the house. Adams, as he would do in the rejoinder, had taken a topic—the crown-realm distinction—on which he thought himself an expert, rather than concentrating on some of the whigs' stronger arguments such as the customary constitution[9] or to ask how the Glorious Revolution, the political event making parliament supreme, could be made binding on the colonies. Adams had preferred to develop a variation of the "original contract" doctrine by seeking intent and purpose in what he understood, at the time the first colonies were settled, was an accepted constitutional principle: that the king and realm of England were distinct. He proved his case by arguments drawn from historical evidence. As a result, Adams had written a brief that would have been easy for Hutchinson to answer if he could disprove the historical accuracy or legal relevancy of Adams's evidence, or if he could overwhelm or neutralize that evidence with counter-evidence leading to opposite legal conclusions.

There is no need to recapitulate John Adams's argument. He did that for us a few years later when he stated the same constitutional theory but based his case on different historical facts.

The first planters of Plymouth were "our ancestors" in the strictest sense. They had no charter or patent for the land they took possession of and derived no authority from the English Parliament or Crown to set up their government. They purchased land of the Indians, and set up a govern-

---

[9]The argument that Americans had obtained their rights to self-government by a century and a half of customary practice was a difficult one for imperialists to answer. It denied parliamentary supremacy by relying on the fact parliament had never claimed it in America. Thus by acquiescence, parliament formulated the constitutional law upon which whig argument relied. "In Accordance with Usage," at 335–68.

ment of their own, on the simple principle of nature, and afterwards purchased a patent for the land of the council at Plymouth, but never purchased any charter for government, of the Crown, or the King, and continued to exercise all the powers of government, legislative, executive and judicial, upon the plain ground of an original contract among independent individuals for 68 years, i.e. until their incorporation with Massachusetts by our present charter. The same may be said of the colonies which emigrated to Saybrook, New-Haven, and other parts of Connecticut. They seem to have had no idea of dependence on Parliament, any more than on the Conclave. The Secretary of Connecticut has now in his possession, an original letter from Charles 2d. to that colony, in which he considers them rather as friendly allies, than as subjects to his English Parliament, and even requests them to pass a law in their assembly, relative to piracy.[10]

In 1773 Adams had not cited the Connecticut precedent, nor did he utilize several others that would have supported his case. He did not, for example, discuss orders issued by James I directing the privy council to investigate the Virginia Company and telling the house of commons not to take up the matter because the privy council was dealing with it.[11] Nor did he mention a petition by the commons to the crown on behalf of the Somers Islands praying relief

[10] Adams, "Novanglus," at 204. "[U]pon complaint of piracies, &c. committed off the coast of Connecticut, King Charles the second, in A.D. 1683-4, instead of causing an act of Parliament to be made to restrain and punish them, writes this letter to the General Assembly in Connecticut, which letter, is now extant in the hands of the Secretary. 'Charles Rex, trusty and well-beloved, we greet you well: Whereas we are informed of great disorders and depredations daily committed, to the prejudice of our allies; contrary to treaties between us and a good correspondence that ought to be maintained between christian princes and states; and we having already given strict order in our Island of Jamaica, against such illegal proceedings, by passing a law for restraining and punishing privateers and pirates, &c. our will and pleasure is, that you take care that such a law (a copy whereof is herewith sent you) be passed within our colony, under your government. . . .' And accordingly the bill was passed into a law by the General Assembly of Connecticut." [Mather,] *America's Appeal*, at 31-32.

[11] Charles Andrews, *Our Earliest Colonial Settlements: Their Diversities of Origin and Later Characteristics* 51 (1971); Arthur Berriedale Keith, *Constitutional History of the First British Empire* 5 (1930).

from a tax imposed by the king's ministers contrary to a promise contained in the colony's charter.[12] The last event could have been a precedent particularly troublesome for Governor Hutchinson. The commons sought relief from prerogative taxation by petition, not by enacting a statute. The legal implication is that it thought the colonies were under the king not under parliament.

We do not know why Adams ignored these precedents. He may not have known about them or he may have concluded that his brief was as long and well documented as necessary. More important is why he did not make use of the historical evidence provided by Thomas Pownall, a former Massachusetts governor, in his well-known pamphlet *The Administration of the Colonies.* The question becomes even more interesting when it is noted that Hutchinson also did not rely on Pownall. The apparent answer tells us much about how these two men selected their authorities. Pownall was highly regarded in London as an expert on colonial governance and his work was the most respected study available. But he could be quoted to support both sides, which may explain why he was cited by neither.

Pownall's interpretation of early American constitutional history fully supported John Adams's case. His research uncovered only two instances before the Restoration when parliament considered legislation for the colonies, and each effort failed.[13] It was not, Pownall concluded, until after the Restoration that the crown shared with parliament power over the colonies.[14] "The Colonies," he argued, had "legislatures peculiar to their own separate communities; subordinate to England, in that they could make no laws contrary to the laws of the mother country; but in all other matters and things, free uncontrouled and compleat legislatures, in conjunction with the King or his deputy as part thereof."[15]

---

[12] Petition of 19 June 1628, 4 *Commons Debates 1628,* at 383–84. The Somers Islands are now Bermuda.

[13] Pownall, *Administration,* at 120–21.

[14] Ibid., at 125.

[15] Ibid., at 139.

They were dominions of the King of England; although, according to the language of those times, "not yet annexed to the crown." They were under the jurisdiction of the King, upon the principles of foedal sovereignty: although considered *"as out of the jurisdiction of the kingdom."* The parliament itself doubting, at that time, whether it had jurisdiction to meddle with those matters, did not think proper to pass bills concerning America.[16]

Pownall, therefore, not only thought pertinent the same historical evidence as did Adams, he came to the same conclusions concerning its constitutional meaning. He then, however, went forward in time and found that the relationship between the colonies and parliament was drastically altered as a result of which the imperial constitution also changed.

When the King, at the restoration, participated this sovereignty over *these his foreign dominions,* with the lords and commons, the Colonies became *in fact,* the dominions of the realm—because subjects of the kingdom.—They came, in fact, and by an actual constitutional exercise of power, under the authority and jurisdiction of parliament. They became connected and annexed to the state: By coming as parts of the British realm, not as a separate kingdom, (which is the case of Ireland) under subjection to the parliament, they became participants of the rights and liberties on which the power of parliament is founded. By the very act of extending the power of parliament over the Colonies, the rights and liberties of the realm must be also extended to them, for, from the nature of the British constitution, from the constitution of parliament itself, they, as parts can be subject by no other mode, than by that in which parliament can exercise its sovereignty; for, the nature of the power, and the nature of the subjection must be recipocal.[17]

Pownall both supported and rejected John Adams's constitutional argument. He agreed that during the reigns of James I and Charles I the North American colonies had been constitutionally independent of parliamentary jurisdic-

[16] Ibid., at 138–39.
[17] Ibid., at 139–40.

tion. He then contended that America's former independence was an historical fact irrelevant to the eighteenth-century constitution, because Charles II had "participated" the lords and commons with his personal sovereignty, making the colonies part of the realm of England. His explanation, however, contributed little to the prerevolutionary controversy because it glossed over some legal issues that troubled whigs and was based on a constitutional premise imperialists could not accept.

John Adams had not adopted Pownall as authority because Pownall's explanation of how parliament came to share sovereignty over the colonies with the king ignored the issue of colonial consent. Looking back much like Hutchinson did at events of the seventeenth century from the perspective of the eighteenth century's sovereign parliament, Pownall gave no heed to how parliament became sovereign. He therefore did not question the legality of one of the parties to the original compact between the first colonial settlers and the king unilaterally altering that compact. Pownall assumed that, when sovereignty was vested in the king and parliament as a unified institution, not only the kingdom but all the dominions of the English empire were bound by its edicts. American whigs could not concede that Pownall was right without abandoning their most fundamental constitutional principle that government rests on the consent of the governed. Pownall assumed a radical alteration in the imperial constitution in which the American role was politically passive. By ignoring the question of colonial consent, he offered a solution that Hutchinson could accept but not the members of the council and house.

Although Pownall did not think the doctrine of consent was relevant to the constitutionality of parliament's assumption of sovereignty over the colonies, he still regarded it as the fundamental principle of the British constitution. When Americans were made part of the realm of England without being accorded representation in parliament, their constitutional right not to be governed or taxed but by consent was violated. This constitutional anomaly had to be corrected and Pownall accompanied his contention that the colonies, at the Restoration, were incorporated into the realm of England with the further argument that they had a constitutional right to elect members to the house of commons.[18] This was a proposition neither whigs nor imperialists could accept, whigs, because colonial representation in parliament could never be on an equal basis, which by American constitutional principles would leave them still unrepresented, imperialists, because it meant that parliament's exercise of jurisdiction over the colonies was currently unconstitutional. It was for this reason that Thomas Hutchinson could not use Pownall's influential and well-known book as an authority. He did not do what we might have expected him to do. That is, he did not dismiss as constitutionally irrelevant Adams's evidence of historical facts from the reigns of the first two Stuarts, and contend, as did Pownall, that when parliament became supreme at home it became supreme throughout the empire. He knew that such an argument, by raising new constitutional considerations, did not solve the constitutional controversy. He would have been asked to state when Americans had consented to "participation" by the lords and commons in the king's sovereignty over the colonies, when Americans had consented to abrogation of the original contract, when Americans had consented to the Glorious Revolution making parliament supreme, and when Americans had been granted representation in parliament. Instead Hutchinson implied the validity of some American constitutional arguments by ignoring the Pownall thesis. Meeting John Adams on his own ground, he disputed the accuracy and relevancy of Adams's historical facts. Hutchinson even offered some contradic-

---

[18] "[A]lthough a right in parliament, to make laws for governing, and taxing the Colonies, may and must, *in the order of time,* precede any right in the Colonies, to a share in the legislature: yet there must arise and proceed pari passu, a right in the Colonies to claim, by petition, a share in the representation, by having knights and burgesses in parliament, by their own election." Pownall, *Administration,* at 141.

tory facts to be set against Adams's evidence. Citing a pamphlet with which he had become familiar while writing his two-volume work, *The History of Massachusetts Bay,* Hutchinson quoted Ferdinando Gorges's statement that he had submitted his claims in North America to the supervision of parliament even though James I was king. Hutchinson's purpose was to show Adams's interpretation of the imperial constitution at the time of settlement to be wrong. If the first settlers went to America knowing they were subject to the supremacy of parliament, and if they acted on that constitutional principle, there would be no need to ask when they had consented to a change in the imperial constitution because that constitution had not been changed. Nor would there be need to ask why they were not represented in parliament. They had always understood and therefore had consented to the reality that they would not be represented.

THE DOCUMENT

On Tuesday the 16th of February *his Excellency was pleased to deliver the following Speech to both Houses in the Council Chamber, viz.*
Gentlemen of the Council, and
Gentlemen of the House of Representatives,
The Proceedings of such of the Inhabitants of the Town of Boston as assembled together and passed and published their Resolves or Votes as the Act of the Town at a legal Town-Meeting, denying in the most express Terms the Supremacy of Parliament, and inviting every other Town and District in the Province to adopt the same Principle and to establish Committees of Correspondence to consult upon proper Measures to maintain it, and the Proceedings of divers other Towns, in Consequence of this Invitation, appeared to me to be so unwarrantable and of such a dangerous Nature and Tendency, that I thought myself bound to call upon you in my Speech at Opening the Session, to join with

me in discountenancing and bearing a proper Testimony against such Irregularities and Innovations.

I stated to you fairly and truly, as I conceived, the Constitution of the Kingdom and of the Province so far as relates to the Dependance of the latter upon the former; and I desired you, if you differed from me in Sentiments, to shew me with Candour my own Errors, and to give your Reasons in support of your Opinions, so far as you might differ from me. I hoped that you would have considered my Speech by your joint Committees, and have given me a joint Answer; but, as the House of Representatives have declined that Mode of Proceeding, and as your Principles in Government are very different, I am obliged to make separate and distinct replies.

I shall first apply myself to you,

Gentlemen of the Council,

The two first Parts of your Answer, which Respect the Disorders occasioned by the Stamp-Act and the general Nature of Supreme Authority, do not appear to me to have a Tendency to invalidate any Thing which I have said in my Speech; for, however the Stamp-Act may have been the immediate Occasion of any Disorders, the Authority of Parliament was notwithstanding denied in Order to justify or excuse them. And, for the Nature of the Supreme Authority of Parliament, I have never given you any Reason to suppose that I intended a more absolute Power in Parliament, or a greater Degree of active or passive Obedience in the People, than what is founded in the Nature of Government, let the Form of it be what it may. I shall, therefore, pass over those Parts of your Answer without any other Remark. I would also have saved you the Trouble of all those Authorities which you have brought to shew, that all Taxes upon English subjects must be levied by Virtue of the Act not of the King alone but in Conjunction with the Lords and Commons, for I should very readily have allowed it; and I should as readily have allowed that all other Acts of Legislation must be passed by the same joint Authority, and not by the King alone.

Indeed, I am not willing to continue a Controversy with you upon any other Parts of your Answer. I am glad to find that Independence is what you have not in Contemplation; and that you will not presume to prescribe the exact Limits of the Authority of Parliament; only, as with due Deference to it, you are humbly of

Opinion, that, as all human Authority in the Nature of it is and ought to be limited, it cannot constitutionally extend for the Reasons you have suggested, to the levying of Taxes in any Form on his Majesty's Subjects of this Province.[1]

I will only observe that your Attempts to draw a Line as the Limits of the Supreme Authority in Government, by distinguishing some natural Rights as more peculiarly exempt from such Authority than the rest, rather tend to evince the Impracticability of drawing such a Line; and that some Parts of your Answer seem to infer a Supremacy in the Province at the same Time that you acknowledge the Supremacy of Parliament, for otherwise the Rights of the Subjects cannot be the same in all essential Respects, as you suppose them to be, in all Parts of the Dominions, "under a like Form of Legislature."

From these, therefore, and other Considerations I cannot help flattering myself, that, upon more mature Deliberation and in Order to a more consistent Plan of Government, you will chuse rather to doubt of the Expediency of Parliament's Exercising its Authority in Cases that may happen, than to limit the Authority itself, especially as you agree with me in the proper Method of obtaining a Redress of Grievances by constitutional Representations, which cannot well consist with a Denial of the Authority to which the Representations are made; and, from the best Information I have been able to obtain, the Denial of the Authority of Parliament, expressly or by Implication in those Petitions to which you refer was the Cause of their not being admitted, and not any Advice given by the Minister to the Agents of the Colonies.

I must enlarge and be much more particular in my Reply to you,

Gentlemen of the House of Representatives,

I shall take no Notice of that Part of your Answer which attributes the Disorders of the Province to an undue Exercise of the Power of Parliament, because you take for granted, what can by no Means be admitted, that Parliament had exercised its Power without just Authority. The Sum of your Answer so far as it is pertinent to my Speech, is this.

---

[1] Hutchinson's meaning is not clear. He was confronting the "two-constitutions" dilemma and may not have understood the issues raised, a possibility he seems to confirm in the next paragraph where he attributes to natural law the council's rejection of the eighteenth-century constitutional foundation of absolute parlia-

You alledge that the Colonies were an Acquisition of Foreign Territory not annexed to the Realm of England, and therefore at the *absolute* Disposal of the Crown; the King having, as you take it, a constitutional Right to dispose of and *alienate* any Part of his Territories not annexed to the Realm—that Queen *Elizabeth* accordingly conveyed the Property, *Dominion* and *Sovereignty* of *Virginia* to Sir *Walter Raleigh* to be held of the Crown *by Homage and a certain Render,* without reserving any Share in the Legislative and Executive Authority—that the subsequent Grants of America were similar in this Respect, that they were without any Reservation for securing the Subjection of the Colonists to the Parliament and future Laws of England,—that this was the Sense of the English Crown, the Nation and our Predecessors when they first took Possession of this Country—that if the Colonies were not then annexed to the Realm they cannot have been annexed since that Time—that if they are not now annexed to the *Realm* they are not Part of the *Kingdom,* and consequently not subject to the Legislative Authority of the Kingdom; for no Country, by the Common Law, was subject to the Laws or to the Parliament but the Realm of England.

Now if this your Foundation shall fail you in every Part of it, as I think it will, the Fabrick which you have raised upon it must certainly fall.

Let me then observe to you that, as English Subjects, and agreeable to the Doctrine of Feudal Tenure, all our Lands and Tenements are held mediately or immediately of the Crown, and although the Possession and Use or Profits be in the Subject, there still remains a Dominion in the Crown. When any new Countries are discovered by English Subjects, according to the general Law and Usage of Nations, they become Part of the State, and, according to the Feudal System, the Lordship or Dominion is in the Crown and a Right accrues of disposing of such Territories, under such Tenure or for such Services to be performed as the Crown shall judge proper, and whensoever any Part of such Territories, by Grant from the Crown, becomes the Possession or

---

mentary supremacy. Yet Hutchinson, himself, acknowledged the validity of the idea government is limited, the foundation of seventeenth-century constitutionalism. It may be that the governor, not understanding the dilemma, did not recognize the inconsistency in his argument. It is also possible that, like other defenders of imperial sovereignty, he attributed American constitutional theories to natural law because he was reluctant to acknowledge their seventeenth-century origins.

Property of private Persons, such Persons, thus holding under the Crown of England, remain or become Subjects of England to all Intents and Purposes, as fully as if any of the Royal Manors Forests or other Territory within the Realm had been granted to them upon the like Tenure. But that it is now, or was when the Plantations were first granted, the Prerogative of the Kings of England to alienate such Territories from the Crown, or to constitute a Number of new Governments altogether independent of the Sovereign Legislative Authority of the English Empire, I can by no Means concede to you. I have never seen any better Authority to support such an Opinion than an anonimous Pamphlet[2] by which I fear you have too easily been mislead, for I shall presently shew you that the Declarations of King James the First, and of King Charles the First, admitting they are truly related by the Author of this Pamphlet,[3] ought to have no Weight with you; nor does the Cession or Restoration, upon a Treaty of Peace, of Countries which have been lost or acquired in War militate with these Principles, nor may any particular Act of Power of a Prince in Selling or delivering up any Part of His Dominions to a foreign Prince or State against the general Sense of the Nation be urged to invalidate them,[4] and upon Examination it will appear that all the Grants which have been made of America are founded upon them and are made to conform to them, even those which you have adduced in Support of very different Principles.

You do not recollect that, prior to what you call the first Grant by Q. Elizabeth to Sir Walter Raleigh, a Grant had been made, by the same Princess, to Sir Humphrey Gilbert of all such Countries as he should discover which were to be *of the Allegiance of her, her*

---

[2] The pamphlet was undoubtedly [Bancroft,] *Remarks.*

[3] As Bancroft cited no authority, Hutchinson was unable to check his accuracy. Had he done so he might have concluded that Charles I never refused his assent to a fishery bill and, therefore, could not have said the words attributed to him by Bancroft and Adams.

[4] A contemporary later quoted from a document that Hutchinson wrote (but did not publish) during the stamp-act crisis that appears to say the opposite: "The right to new acquired countries, according to the constitution of England, two hundred years ago, was allowed to be in the crown. The crown from time to time disposed of these countries not only to their own subjects, but to foreign princes: particularly *Acadia* and *Nova-Scotia,* when begun to be settled by British subjects, were ceded to *France,* although France had no better claim to them than New-England: and *Surinam* was sold to, or exchanged with the *Dutch.*" Gordon, *Revolution,* at 125.

Heirs and Successors but, he dying in the Prosecution of his Voyage, a second Grant was made to Sir Walter Raleigh which, you say, conveyed the Dominion and Sovereignty without any Reserve of Legislative or Executive Authority *being held by Homage and a Render.*[5] To hold by *Homage,* which implies Fealty, *and a Render* is Descriptive of Socage Tenure as fully as if it had been said to hold *as of our Manor of East Greenwich* the Words in your Charter. Now this alone was a Reserve of Dominion and Sovereignty in the Queen her Heirs and Successors and, besides this, the Grant is made upon this express Condition, which you pass over, *that the People remain subject to the Crown of England,* the Head of that Legislative Authority which, by the English Constitution, is equally extensive with the Authority of the Crown throughout every Part of the Dominions.[6] Now if we could suppose the Queen to have acquired separate from her Relations to her Subjects, or in her natural Capacity, which she could not do, a Title to a Country discovered by her Subjects and then to grant the same Country to English Subjects in her publick Capacity as Queen of England, still by this Grant she annexed it to the Crown. Thus by not distinguishing between the Crown of England and the Kings and Queens of England in their personal or natural Capacities, you have been led into a fundamental Error which must prove fatal to your System. It is not material whether Virginia reverted to the Crown by Sir Walter's Attainder or whether he never took any Benefit from his Grant, though the latter is most probable seeing he ceased from all Attempts to take Possession of the Country after a few Years Trial. There were, undoubtedly, divers Grants made by King James the First of the Continent of America in the Beginning of the 17th Century and similar to the Grant of Queen Elizabeth in this Respect, that they were dependent on the Crown. The Charter to the Council at Plimouth in Devon dated November 3d. 1620 more immediately respects us, and of that we have the most authentick Remains.

By this Charter, upon the Petition of Sir Ferdinando Gorges a

[5] John Adams may have made this mistake because he was following Bancroft who, correcting a statement by William Knox, insisted that the first charter was not granted by King James but by Elizabeth to Raleigh. [Bancroft,] *Remarks,* at 11.

[6] In fact, the form of tenure in which the colonies were granted was irrelevant to the question of the queen's interest concerning sovereignty and supremacy. Tenure, selected with an eye on private not public law, determined the relationship of the grantee to the crown regarding matters such as feudal dues to be paid.

Corporation was constituted to be and continue by Succession for-
ever in the Town of Plimouth aforesaid, to which Corporation
that Part of the American Continent which lies between the 40°
and 48° Degrees of Latitude was granted *to be held of the King and
his Heirs and Successors as of the Manor of East Greenwich* with Powers
to constitute subordinate Governments in America and to make
Laws for such Governments, *not repugnant to the Laws and Statutes
of England.* From this Corporation your Predecessors obtained a
Grant of the Soil of the Colony of Massachusets-Bay, in 1627,
and, in 1628, they obtained a Charter from King Charles the First
making them a distinct Corporation, also within the Realm, and
giving them full Powers within the Limits of their Patent, very like
to those of the Council of Plimouth throughout their more extensive Territory.

We will now consider what must have been the Sense of the
King of the Nation and of the Patentees at the Time of granting
these Patents. From the Year 1602 the Banks and Sea Coasts of
New-England had been frequented by English Subjects for catch-
ing and drying Cod-Fish. When an exclusive Right to the Fishery
was claimed, by Virtue of the Patent of 1620, the House of Commons was alarmed and a Bill was brought in for allowing a free
Fishery, and it was upon this Occasion that one of the Secretaries
of State declared perhaps as his own Opinion, that the Plantations
were not annexed to the Crown and so were not within the Jurisdiction of Parliament. Sir Edwin Sandys, who was one of the Virginia Company and an eminent Lawyer, declared that he knew
Virginia had been annexed and *was held of the Crown as of the
Manor of East Greenwich* and he believed New-England was so
also;[7] and so it most certainly was. This Declaration, made by one
of the King's Servants, you say shewed the Sense of the Crown
and, being not secretly but openly declared in Parliament you
would make it the Sense of the Nation also, notwithstanding your
own Assertion that the Lords and Commons passed a Bill that
shewed their Sense to be directly the contrary. But if there had
been full Evidence of express Declarations made by King James
the First, and King Charles the First, they were Declarations contrary to their own Grants, which declare this Country to be held
of the Crown and consequently it must have been annexed to it.
And may not such Declarations be accounted for by other Actions

---

[7] Hutchinson's evidence is discussed below, at the end of the replication.

of those Princes who when they were solliciting the Parliament to grant the Duties of Tonnage and Poundage with other Aids and were, in this Way, acknowledging the Rights of Parliament, at the same Time were requiring the Payment of those Duties with Ship Money, &c. by Virtue of their Prerogative?[8]

But to remove all doubt of the Sense of the Nation and of the Patentees of this Patent or Charter in 1620 I need only refer you to the Account published by Sir Ferdinando Gorges himself of the Proceedings in Parliament upon this Occasion. As he was the most active Member of the Council of Plimouth and as he relates what came within his own Knowledge and Observation his Narrative, which has all the Appearance of Truth and Sincerity, must carry Conviction with it. He says that soon after the Patent was passed and whilst it lay in the Crown-Office he was summoned to appear in Parliament to answer what was to be objected against it, and the House being in a Committee and Sir Edward Coke that great Oracle of the Law, in the Chair, he was called to the Bar and was told by Sir Edward that the House understood that a Patent had been granted to the said Sir Ferdinando and divers other noble Persons for establishing a Colony in New-England, that this was deemed a Grievance of the Common-wealth *contrary to the Laws,* and to the Privileges of the Subject, that it was a Monopoly, &c. and he required the Delivery of the Patent into the House.[9] Sir Ferdinando Gorges made no Doubt of the Authority

[8] Hutchinson was using history to establish an important legal point. The house had cited the grants of certain kings to prove the intent of the crown and of the first American settlers (the grantees) at the time the grants were made: that the parties intended that the colonies would not be subject to the authority of parliament. In this paragraph Hutchinson reminded the house that those kings were the same ones who attempted to rule at home without parliament by exercising prerogative taxation. They had failed to establish that power. Parliament became supreme in the area of taxation. Hutchinson attempted to link the asserted royal claim to grant the colonies autonomy from parliament with the royal attempt to tax by prerogative right and brush the first with the unconstitutional hue of the second. Again, ignoring the two-constitution dilemma, he assumed that actions that had become unconstitutional should be seen as having always been unconstitutional, an anachronism common among eighteenth-century lawyers.

[9] On behalf of the house of commons Sir Edward Coke informed Gorges "that the House understood that there was a Patent granted to me, and diverse other noble persons therein nominated for the establishing of a Colony in *New England,* this (as it seemes) was a grievance of the *Common-wealth,* and so complained of in respect to many particulars therein contained contrary to the Lawes and priviledges of the subjects, as also that it was a Monopoly, and the colour of planting a

of the House but submitted to their Disposal of the Patent as in their Wisdom they thought good "not knowing, under Favour, how any Action of that Kind could be a Grievance to the Publick seeing it was undertaken for the Advancement of Religion, *the Enlargement of the Bounds of our Nation,* &c.[10] He was willing, however, to submit the whole to their honorable Censures."[11] After divers Attendances he imagined he had satisfied the House that the planting a Colony was of much more Consequence than a simple disorderly Course of Fishing. He was, notwithstanding, disappointed and, when the Publick Grievances of the Kingdom were presented by the two Houses, that of the Patent for New-England was the first.[12] I don't know how the Parliament could have shewn more fully the Sense they then had of their Authority over this new acquired Territory, nor can we expect better Evidence of the Sense which the Patentees had of it, for I know of no historical Fact of which we have less Reason to doubt.

And now Gentlemen I will shew you how it appears from our Charter itself, which you say I have not yet been pleased to point out to you except from that Clause which restrains us from making Laws repugnant to the Laws of England, that it was the Sense of our Predecessors at the Time when the Charter was granted that they were to remain subject to the Supreme Authority of Parliament.

Besides this Clause, which I shall have Occasion further to re-

---

Colony put upon it for particular ends, and private gaine, which the House was to look unto and to Minister justice to all parties . . . but before they could descend to other matters in the businesse, the Patent was to be brought unto the House, therefore the delivery of it." Gorges, *A Briefe Narration,* at 36–37; Gorges, *Description of New-England,* at 66–67.

[10] Gorges, *A Briefe Narration,* at 37; Gorges, *Description of New-England,* at 67.

[11] Gorges, *A Briefe Narration,* at 39; Gorges, *Description of New-England* at 68.

[12] These patents were made grievances that the king was asked to remedy. "Sir *Edward Cooke* [*i.e.,* Coke] saith, that the House did condemn, at the last Meeting, Nineteen several *Patents,* for Grievances, both in Creation and Execution; and that his Majesty since, by his Proclamation, hath decried Thirteen of these Patents; so as there remain still Six Patents of the Nineteen, which are yet undecried: *viz.* I. The patent for the sole bringing in of Lobsters and Salmon." Debate of 17 December 1621, 2 [Nicholas,] *Proceedings of 1620–21,* at 347–48. Explaining the constitutional theory, Coke said, "that since there are so many Grievances here in the House complained of, (being, at the least, Twenty-three in Number) as that we cannot make Laws against them all, that we should have a Petition made to the King, beseeching his Majesty to be pleased, by a Proclamation or otherwise, to decry, or make void the same. . . ." Debate of 29 November 1621, ibid., at 248.

mark upon before I finish, you will find that, by the Charter a Grant was made of Exemption from all Taxes and Impositions upon any Goods imported *into New-England,* or exported from thence into England for the Space of twenty-one Years, except the Custom of five per Cent upon such Goods as, after the Expiration of seven Years, should be brought into England. Nothing can be more plain than that the Charter, as well as the Patent to the Council of Plimouth, constitutes a Corporation in England with Powers to create a subordinate Government or Governments within the Plantation, so that there would always be Subjects of Taxes and Impositions both in the Kingdom and in the Plantation. An Exemption for twenty-one Years implies a Right of Imposition after the Expiration of the Term, and there is no Distinction between the Kingdom and the Plantation. By what Authority, then, in the Understanding of the Parties, were these Impositions to be laid?[13] If any, to support a System, should say by the King rather than to acknowledge the Authority of Parliament, yet this could not be the Sense of one of our principal Patentees Mr. Samuel Vassall who at that Instant, 1628, the Date of the Charter, was suffering the Loss of his Goods rather than submit to an Imposition laid by the King without the Authority of Parliament;[14] and to prove that a few Years after it could not be the Sense of the rest, I need only to refer you to your own Records for the Year 1642 where you will find an Order of the House of Commons, conceived in such Terms as discover a plain Reference to this Part of the Charter, after fourteen Years of the Twenty-one were expired. By this Order the House of Commons declare that all Goods and Merchandize exported to New-England or imported from thence shall be free from all Taxes and Impositions both in the Kingdom *and in New-England* until the House shall take fur-

[13] As noted previously American whigs would not have thought this exemption from taxation relevant, as custom had established it as part of the regulation of imperial trade, a function that on one basis (*i.e.,* consent) or another (*i.e.,* necessity) Americans conceded to the superintendance of parliament.

[14] Hutchinson confused the constitutional argument. Vassall's actions were not pertinent to the imperial case because the argument in 1628 had not been whether parliament or the king could tax. It had been about whether the king alone, by prerogative right, could impose taxation without consent of parliament. Vassall (and others) appealed to "constitutional laws," "common law," "magna carta," "fundamental law," etc. against the assertions of the crown. He did not appeal to parliamentary supremacy. Put another way, he appealed to the same law to which Americans 140 years later would appeal.

ther Order therein to the contrary. The Sense which our Predecessors had of the Benefit which they took from this Order
evidently appears from the Vote of the General Court,
acknowledging their humble Thankfulness, and preserving a
grateful Remembrance of the Honorable Respect from that high
Court, and resolving that the Order sent unto them under the
Hand of the Clerk of the Honorable House of Commons shall be
entered among their Publick Records to remain there unto Posterity: And, in an Address to Parliament, Nine Years after, they
acknowledge, among other undeserved Favours that of *taking off
the Customs from them.*

I am at a Loss to know what your Ideas could be when you say
that if the Plantations are not Part of the *Realm,* they are not Part
of the *Kingdom,* seeing the two Words can properly convey but
one Idea and they have one and the same Signification in the
different Languages from whence they are derived. I do not
charge you with any Design, but the equivocal Use of the Word
Realm in several Parts of your Answer makes them perplexed and
obscure. Sometimes, you must intend the whole Dominion which
is subject to the Authority of Parliament, sometimes only strictly
the Territorial Realm to which other Dominions are or may be
annexed. If you mean that no Countries but the ancient territorial
Realm can constitutionally be subject to the Supreme Authority of
England, which you have very incautiously said is a Rule of the
Common Law of England, this is Doctrine which you will never
be able to support.[15] That the Common Law should be controuled
and changed by Statutes every Day's Experience teaches, but that
the Common Law prescribes Limits to the Extent of the Legislative Power, I believe has never been said upon any other Occasion. That Acts of Parliament for several Hundred Years past
have respected Countries, which are not strictly within the Realm,
you might easily have discovered by the Statute Books. You will
find Acts for regulating the Affairs of Ireland, though a separate
and distinct Kingdom. Wales and Calais, whilst they sent no Representatives to Parliament, were subject to the like Regulations. So

[15] This statement helped provide the only direct evidence we have that both of
the Adamses contributed to these documents. Samuel wrote to John: "The
Gov[erno]r says the House have *incautiously* applied a rule of the Common Law.
. . . The Assertion is *mine,* upon *your* Authority, as I thought. If it be vindicable,
pray give me your Aid in that as briefly as you please." Letter from Samuel Adams
to John Adams, n.d., 2 Adams, *Writings,* at 430.

are Guernsey, Jersey, Alderney, &c. which send no Members to this Day. These Countries are not more properly a Part of the ancient Realm, than the Plantations, nor do I know that they can more properly be said to be annexed to the Realm, unless the declaring that Acts of Parliament shall extend to Wales, though not particularly named shall make it so, which I conceive it does not in the Sense you intend.

Thus, I think, I have made it appear that the Plantations, though not strictly within the Realm, have from the Beginning been constitutionally subject to the Supreme Authority of the Realm and are so far annexed to it as to be, with the Realm and the other Dependencies upon it, one intire Dominion; and that the Plantation or Colony of Massachusetts-Bay in particular is holden as feudatory of the Imperial Crown of England: Deem it to be no Part of the Realm it is immaterial, for, to use the Words of a very great Authority[16] in a Case in some Respects analogous, "being Feudatory the Conclusion necessary follows, that it is under the Government of the King's Laws and the King's Courts in Cases proper for them to interpose, though (like Counties Palatine) it has peculiar Laws and Customs, Jura Regalia, and complete Jurisdiction at Home."[17]

Your Remark upon and Construction of the Words, *not Repugnant to the Laws of England,* are much the same with those of the Council; but can any Reason be assigned why the Laws of England as they stood just at that Period should be pitched upon as the Standard, more than at any other Period? If so, why was it not recur[r]ed to when the second Charter was Granted, more than sixty Years after the first? It is not improbable that the original Intention might be a Repugnancy in general and, a Fortiori, such Laws as were made more immediately to Respect us, but the statute of 7th and 8th, of King William and Queen Mary, soon after the second Charter, favours the latter Construction only, and the Province Agent, Mr. Dummer, in his much applauded Defence of the Charter, says that *then* a Law in the Plantations may be said to be repugnant to a Law made in Great Britain, when it flatly contradicts it so far as the Law made there mentions and

[16] Lord Mansfield.
[17] The case involved Berwick which the defendant claimed was conquered territory, not incorporated into the realm of England and, therefore, beyond the jurisdiction of common-law writs. Mansfield rejected the argument. Rex v. Cowle, 2 *Burrows Reports* 834, 851 (1759).

relates to the Plantations.[18] But, Gentlemen, there is another Clause both in the first and second Charter which, I think will serve to explain this or to render all Dispute upon the Construction of it unnecessary.—You are enabled to impose such Oaths only as are warrantable by, or not repugnant to the Laws and Statutes of the Realm. I believe you will not contend that these Clauses must mean such Oaths only as were warrantable at the respective Times when the Charters were granted. It has often been found necessary, since the Date of the Charters, to alter the Forms of the Oaths to the Government by Acts of Parliament, and such Alterations have always been conformed to in the Plantations.

Lest you should think that I admit the Authority of King Charles the Second in giving his Assent to an Act of the Assembly of Virginia, which you subjoin to the Authorities of James the First and Charles the First, to have any Weight, I must observe to you that I do not see any greater Inconsistency with Magna Charta in the King's giving his Assent to an Act of a Subordinate Legislature immediately or in Person than when he does it mediately by his Governor or Substitute but, if it could be admitted that such an Assent discovered the King's Judgment that Virginia was Independent, would you lay any Stress upon it when the same King was from Time to Time giving his Assent to Acts of Parliament which inferred the Dependence of all the Colonies, and had by one of those Acts declared the Plantations to be inhabited and peopled by his Majesty Subjects of England?

I gave you no Reason to Remark upon the Absurdity of a Grant to Persons born within the Realm of the same Liberties which would have belonged to them if they had been born within the Realm, but rather guarded against it by considering such Grant as declaratory only, and in the Nature of an Assurance that the Plantations would be considered as the Dominions of England. But is there no Absurdity in a Grant from the King of England of the Liberties and Immunities of Englishmen to Persons born in and who are to inhabit other Territories than the Dominions of England, and would such Grant, whether by Charter or other Letters Patent, be sufficient to make them inheritable, or to intitle them to the other Liberties and Immunities of Englishmen, in any Part of the English Dominions?

[18] Dummer, *Defence of the Charters*, at 30.

As I am willing to rest the Point between us upon the Plantations having been, from their first Discovery and Settlement under the Crown, a Part of the Dominions of England, I shall not take up any Time in remarking upon your Arguments to shew that since that Time, they cannot have been made a Part of those Dominions.

The remaining Parts of your Answer are principally intended to prove that, under both Charters, it hath been the Sense of the People that they were not subject to the Jurisdiction of Parliament, and, for this Purpose, you have made large Extracts from the History of the Colony. Whilst you are doing Honor to the Book, by laying any Stress upon its Authority, it would have been no more than Justice to the Author if you had cited some other Passages which would have tended to reconcile the Passage, in my Speech to the History. I have said that, except about the Time of the Anarchy which preceded the Restoration of King Charles the Second, I have not discovered that the Authority of Parliament had been called in Question even by particular Persons. It was, as I take it, from the Principles imbibed in those Times of Anarchy that the Persons of Influence, mentioned in the History, disputed the Authority of Parliament, but the Government would not venture to dispute it. On the contrary, in four or five Years after the Restoration, the Government declared to the King's Commissioners that the Act of Navigation had been for some Years observed here, that they knew not of it's being greatly violated and that such Laws as appeared to be against it were repealed, It is not strange that these Persons of Influence should prevail upon great Part of the People to fall in, for a Time with their Opinions and to suppose Acts of the Colony necessary to give Force to Acts of Parliament; the Government, however, several Years before the Charter was vacated, more explicitly acknowledged the Authority of Parliament and voted that their Governor should take the Oath, required of him, faithfully to do and perform all Matters and Things enjoined him by the Acts of Trade.[19] I have not recited in my Speech all these Particulars, nor had I them all in my Mind but, I think, I have said nothing inconsistent with them. My Principles in Government are still the same with what they appear to be in the Book you refer to, nor am I conscious that, by any Part of my Conduct, I have given Cause to suggest the contrary.

[19] 12 Charles II, cap. 18, sec. 2.

Inasmuch as you say that I have not particularly pointed out to you the Acts and Doings of the General Assembly which relate to Acts of Parliament, I will do it now, and demonstrate to you that such Acts have been acknowledged by the Assembly, or submitted to by the People.

From your Predecessors Removal to America until the Year 1640 there was no Session of Parliament and the first short Session of a few Days only in 1640, and the whole of the next Session, until the withdraw of the King, being taken up in the Disputes between the King and the Parliament, there could be no Room for Plantation Affairs. Soon after the King's withdraw the House of Commons passed the memorable Order of 1642,[20] and from that Time to the Restoration, this Plantation seems to have been distinguished from the rest, and the several Acts or Ordinances, which respected the other Plantations, were never enforced here, and, possibly, under Colour of the Exemption in 1642, it might not be intended they should be executed.

For 15 or 16 Years after the Restoration, there was no Officer of the Customs in the Colony, except the Governor annually elected by the People, and the Acts of Trade were but little regarded, nor did the Governor take the Oath required of Governors by the Act of the 12th of King Charles the Second, until the Time which I have mentioned. Upon the Revolution the Force of an Act of Parliament was evident in a Case of as great Importance as any which could happen to the Colony. King William and Queen Mary were proclaimed in the Colony, King and Queen of England, France and Ireland, *and the Dominions thereunto belonging,* in the Room of King James, and this not by Virtue of an Act of the Colony, for no such Act ever passed, but by Force of an Act of Parliament which altered the Succession to the Crown, and for which the People waited several Weeks with anxious Concern.[21] By Force of another Act of Parliament, and that only, such Officers of the Colony as had taken the Oaths of Allegiance to King

[20] 1 Hutchinson, *Massachusetts Bay,* at 99–100.

[21] This argument attempted to resolve what was the most difficult question faced by imperialists who contended that parliament possessed the supreme law-making power over the colonies. Parliament had become supreme in England (as the Scots parliament had become supreme in Scotland) when it replaced James II and elected William and Mary to the throne. But how did it become supreme over the colonies? Hutchinson's explanation is colonial acquiescence or adoption by implication.

James deemed themselves at Liberty to take, and accordingly did take the Oaths to King William and Queen Mary. And that I may mention other Acts of the like Nature together, it is by Force of an Act of Parliament that the Illustrious House of Hanover succeeded to the Throne of Britain *and its Dominions,* and by several other Acts, the Forms of the Oaths have from Time to Time, been altered, and by a late Act that Form was established which every one of us has complied with as the Charter in express Words requires and makes our Duty. Shall we now dispute whether Acts of Parliament have been submitted to when we find them submitted to in Points which are of the very Essence of our Constitution? If you should disown that Authority which has Power even to change the Succession to the Crown, are you in no Danger of denying the Authority of our most gracious Sovereign, which I am sure none of you can have in your Thoughts?

I think I have before shewn you, Gentlemen, what must have been the Sense of our Predecessors at the time of the first Charter, let us now, whilst we are upon the Acts and Doings of the Assembly, consider what it must have been at the Time of the second Charter. Upon the first Advice of the Revolution in England, the Authority which assumed the Government instructed their Agents to petition *the Parliament* to restore the first Charter, and a Bill for that Purpose passed the House of Commons, but went no farther. Was not this owning *the Authority of Parliament?* By an Act of Parliament, passed in the first Year of King William and Queen Mary, a Form of Oaths was established to be taken by those Princes and by all succeeding Kings and Queens of England at their Coronation, the first of which is, that they will govern the People of the Kingdom *and the Dominions thereunto belonging, according to the Statutes in Parliament agreed on, and the Laws and Customs of the same.* When the Colony directed their Agents to make their humble Application to King William to grant the second Charter, they could have no other Pretence than as they were Inhabitants of Part *of the Dominions of England,* and they also knew the Oath the King had taken to govern them *according to the Statutes in Parliament;* surely then, at the Time of this Charter also, it was the Sense of our Predecessors, as well as of the King and of the Nation that there was and would remain a Supremacy in the Parliament. About the same Time, they acknowledge, in an Address to the King, that they have no Power to make Laws *repugnant to the Laws of England.* And, immediately after the Assumption of the Powers of Government by Virtue of the new Charter, an Act passed to revive for a limited Time all the Local Laws of the Colonies of Massachusetts-Bay and New-Plimouth, respectively, *not repugnant to the Laws of England.*[22] And, at the same Session, an Act passed establishing Naval Officers in several Ports of the Province, for which this Reason is given, *that all undue Trading contrary to an Act of Parliament made in the 15th Year of King Charles the Second may be prevented in this their Majesty's Province.*[23] The Act of this Province passed so long ago as the second Year of King George the first, for stating the Fees of the Custom-House Officers, must have relation to the Acts of Parliament by which they are constituted, and the Provision made in that Act of the Province for extending the Port of Boston to all the Roads as far as Cape-Cod, could be for no other Purpose than for the more effectual carrying the Acts of Trade into Execution.[24] And, to come nearer to the present Time, when an Act of Parliament had passed in 1741, for putting an End to certain unwarrantable Schemes in this Province, did the Authority of Government, or those Persons more immediately affected by it, ever dispute the Validity of it? On the contrary, have not a Number of Acts been passed in the Province, that the Burdens to which such Persons were subjected might be equally apportioned, and have not all those Acts of the Province been very carefully framed to prevent their militating with the Act of Parliament? I will mention also an Act of Parliament made in the first Year of Queen Ann, altho' the Proceedings upon it more immediately respected the Council. By this Act no Office Civil or Military shall be void by the Death of the King, but shall continue six Months, unless suspended or made void by the next Successor. By force of this Act, Governor Dudley continued in the Administration six Months from the Demise of Queen Ann, and immediately after, the Council assumed the Administration and continued it until a Proclamation arrived from King George, by Virtue of which Governor Dudley reassumed the Government. It would be tedious to enumerate the Addresses, Votes and Messages of both the Council and House of

[22] "That all the local laws . . . being not repugnant to the laws of England nor inconsistent with the present constitution and settlement by their majesties' royal charter, do remain and continue in full force. . . ." Chapter 1, Acts of 1692, 1 *Acts and Resolves*, at 27.

[23] Chapter 6, Acts of 1692, *ibid.*, at 34.

[24] Chapter 6, Acts of 1716/17, 2 *Acts and Resolves*, at 44–45.

Representatives to the same Purpose. I have said enough to shew that this Government has submitted to Parliament from a Conviction of it's constitutional Supremacy, and this not *from Inconsideration, nor meerly from Reluctance at the Idea of contending with the Parent State.*

If then I have made it appear, that both by the first and second Charters we hold our Lands and the Authority of Government not of the *King* but of the *Crown* of England, that being a Dominion of the Crown of England, we are consequently subject to the Supreme Authority of England, that this hath been the Sense of this Plantation, except in those few Years when the Principles of Anarchy which had prevailed in the Kingdom had not lost their Influence here; and if, upon a Review of your Principles, they shall appear to you to have been delusive and erroneous, as I think they must, or if you shall only be in Doubt of them, you certainly will not draw that Conclusion which otherwise you might do, and which I am glad you have hitherto avoided; especially when you consider the obvious and inevitable Distress and Misery of Independence upon our Mother Country, if such Independence could be allowed or maintained, and the Probability of much greater Distress, which we are not able to foresee.

You ask me if we have not Reason to fear we shall soon be reduced to a worse Situation than that of the Colonies of France, Spain or Holland. I may safely affirm that we have not; that we have no Reason to Fear any Evils from a Submission to the Authority of Parliament, equal to what we must feel from its Authority being disputed, from an uncertain Rule of Law and Government. For more than seventy Years together the Supremacy of Parliament was acknowledged without Complaints of Grievance. The Effect of every Measure cannot be foreseen by human Wisdom. What can be expected more from any Authority than when the Unfitness of a Measure is discovered, to make it void? When upon the united Representations and Complaints of the American Colonies any Acts have appeared to Parliament to be unsalutary, have there not been repeated Instances of the Repeal of such Acts? We cannot expect these Instances should be carried so far as to be equivalent to a Disavowal or Relinquishment of the Right itself. Why then shall we fear for ourselves and our Posterity, greater rigour of Government for seventy Years to come than what we and our Predecessors have felt in the seventy Years past.

You must give me Leave, Gentlemen, in a few Words to vindicate myself from a Charge, in one Part of your Answer, of having, by my Speech, reduced you to the unhappy Alternative of appearing by your Silence to acquiesce in my Sentiments, or of freely discussing this Point of the Supremacy of Parliament. I saw, as I have before observed, the Capital Town of the Province, without being reduced to such an Alternative, voluntarily not only discussing but determining this Point, and inviting every other Town and District in the Province to do the like. I saw that many of the principal Towns had followed the Example, and that there was imminent Danger of a Compliance in most if not all the Rest, in Order to avoid being distinguished. Was not I reduced to the Alternative of rendering myself justly obnoxious to the Displeasure of my Sovereign by acquiesing in such Irregularities, or of calling upon you to join with me in suppressing them? Might I not rather have expected from you an Expression of your Concern that any Persons should project and prosecute a Plan of Measures which would lay me under a Necessity of bringing this Point before you? It was so far from being my Inclination, that nothing short of a Sense of Duty to the King, and the Obligations I am under to consult your true Interest could have compelled me to it.

Gentlemen of the Council, and
Gentlemen of the House of Representatives,

We all profess to be the loyal and dutiful Subjects of the King of Great-Britain. His Majesty considers the British Empire as one entire Dominion, subject to one Supreme Legislative Power, a due Submission to which is essential to the Maintenance of the Rights, Liberties, and Privileges of the several Parts of this Dominion. We have abundant Evidence of his Majesty's tender and impartial Regard to the Rights of his Subjects; and I am authorized to say that "his Majesty will most graciously approve of every Constitutional Measure that may contribute to the Peace, the Happiness, and Prosperity of his Colony of Massachusetts-Bay, and which may have the Effect to shew to the World that he has no wish beyond that of reigning in the Hearts and Affections of his People."

HISTORICAL EVIDENCE AND THE REPLICATION

INTRODUCTION

Before considering the council's rejoinder, it would be beneficial to ask about the accuracy of the historical evidence that John Adams cited in the answer of the house and that Thomas Hutchinson rejected in his replication. Adams, it will be recalled, asserted that "James the First," addressing the commons, "declared . . . that America *was not annexed to the Realm,* and it was not fitting that Parliament should make Laws for those Countries." Hutchinson attempted to overcome this evidence by questioning its accuracy and by discrediting it with counterevidence showing that the commons, in the case of Ferdinando Gorges, demonstrated that they did not accept James's edict.

Recently, experts on the writings of John Adams have suggested that his source for the words of James I was the book by Thomas Pownall previously discussed.[1] If so, Adams took liberties with the text for Pownall did not quite say what Adams claims. "[W]hen the House of Commons," Pownall wrote, "in those reiterated attempts which they made by passing a bill to get a law enacted for establishing

---

[1] *Papers of John Adams,* at 330n2.

a free right of fishery on the coasts of Virginia, New-England, and Newfoundland, put in the claim of the state to this property, and of the parliament to jurisdiction over it; they were told in the House by the servants of the crown, 'That it was not fit to make laws here for those countries which are not yet annexed to the crown.' 'That this bill was not proper for this house, as it concerneth America.' Nay, it was doubted by others, 'whether the house had jurisdiction to meddle with these matters.' "[2] As authority for these quotations, Pownall cited the *Journal of the House of Commons* for 25 and 29 April 1621. Unfortunately for his accuracy, the house did not meet on 29 April. It did, however, meet on 25 April. That was the day that the commons took under consideration "An Act for the freer Liberty of Fishing, and Fishing Voyages, to be made and performed on the Sea-coasts and Places of *New-found-land, Virginia,* and *New England,* and other Coasts and Parts of *America.*" There was a rather lengthy discussion in the course of which "Mr. Secretary" said that he "Doubteth, the Fishermen [were] the Hinderers of the Plantation.—That they burn great Store of Woods and choak the Havens.—Never will strain the King's Prerogative against the Good of the Commonwealth.—Not fit to make any Laws here for those Countries, which not as yet annexed to this Crown." The debate continued and after three others spoke Sir John Brooke was quoted, apparently in answer to the secretary, "That we may make Laws here for *Virginia;* for, if the King give Consent to this Bill, passed here, and by the Lords, this will controul the Patent. The Case diverse for *Gascoigne, &c.* which Principality of themselves. To commit it." Finally Sir Edward "Sands" made the observation "That *Virginia* [is] holden of the Manor of *East Greenwich,*" and the bill was committed to a subcommittee.[3]

It seems evident that a copy of the *Journal of the House of Commons* was not available in Massachusetts Bay, as neither Adams nor Hutchinson cited it. It also is apparent that Pownall was not Adams's authority for the sayings of James

[2] Pownall, *Administration,* at 48–49.
[3] *Journal of the House of Commons,* 19 James I, 25 April 1621.

I. For one thing, Pownall's book was not anonymous, and Hutchinson said Adams used an anonymous pamphlet. For another, it seems quite unlikely that Adams would not have quoted all that Pownall said if that was his source. The other quotations would have strengthened his case.

The fact is that Adams cribbed not from Pownall but from Edward Bancroft. Even with this source Adams was not accurate. Bancroft had the very words that Adams quoted, but he attributed them not to James I as did Adams, but to a subordinate official. "[T]he House," he wrote of the commons, "was told by the Secretary of State, from his Majesty, that *America* was not annexed to the Realm, and that it was not fitting that Parliament should make Laws for those Countries."[4]

It is probably indicative of the haste under which the briefs were written that Governor Hutchinson did not embarrass Adams by calling attention to how he took the words that Bancroft had attributed to the secretary of state and put them in the mouth of James I. Even more indicative of the pressure on both men is the fact that they did not go to the *Journal of the House of Commons* for evidence of what was said. As just suggested, they probably did not have a copy of the *Journal* itself, but that might not have been a material fact. One of the most important of the prerevolutionary pamphlets, published three years before by William Knox, contained extracts from the *Journal* much more extensive than those just quoted.[5] Knox printed everything said in the commons about the fishing bill, using the evidence to reach a constitutional conclusion that Hutchinson surely would not have overlooked had he not been working alone and pressed for time. There is no need to repeat Knox's extracts. His conclusion summarizes the evidence of which Hutchinson might have made much had it come to his attention.

[T]he doubts of *the right of parliament to make laws to bind the Colonies,* was raised by the *king's secretary,* and that the *only members* of the house of commons, who seemed to doubt

---

[4] [Bancroft], *Remarks,* at 23–24.
[5] [Knox,] *Controversy* (Appendix), at vii–xviii.

along with him, were *two of the patentees*,[6] Mr. Smith and Mr. Guy. The majority of the commons, were so far from doubting of their jurisdiction, that they passed the bill, which occasioned the doubt, which was not only *asserting* their right, but actually *exercising* it, as far as any house of parliament can exercise any legislative jurisdiction. And what is still more, the secretary and the patentees seem to have not only *acquiesced* in the right claimed by parliament, but to have been drawn over to the opinion, that parliament had such a right, for in the progress of the bill, we find them silent upon the matter of right, and complaining of the hardships imposed by it on the Settlers, by authorising and giving a right to English fishermen to *cut down timber* off *their lands,* and without paying them for it, even within a quarter of a mile of their houses: And proposing some amendments in favour of the colonists: *Without which,* Mr. Secretary says, he *doubts* whether the bill will receive the royal assent. But these commons of England were not to be led by the king's secretary from their duty to the state; they rejected the provisoes; upon this truly parliamentary reason, "that the fishing was more beneficial to the *commonwealth* than the plantation."[7]

Were we to examine the evidence impartially, it might be concluded that imperialist William Knox had overstated his conclusion at least as much as had whig Edward Bancroft. There is, however, no need to speculate. It is possible for us to make individual assessments, as several reports of the commons debates, besides the *Journal of the House of Commons,* are extant. Interestingly, one of them, *Nicholas Proceedings,* had been published in 1766 and therefore certainly was available to Knox and Bancroft who were in London when they wrote, although, as neither cited it, we must assume it was not available to Hutchinson and Adams. The other extant reports, of which there are four, remained manuscripts until the twentieth century. Although these sources could not have been quoted in 1773 they are still of interest, as they shed light on the reliability of evidence

---

[6] That is, two of the grantees of the charter to the Virginia Company who, of course, opposed parliamentary interference with their patent.

[7] [Knox,] *Controversy,* at 147–48.

once cited to settle constitutional disputes. It must be remembered that participants in prerevolutionary debates thought that what was said by King James or by members speaking on the floor of the commons was not only relevant, it was conclusive. The question to be asked today is whether evidence of this sort could ever be relevant let alone conclusive.

NICHOLAS PROCEEDINGS

Concerning the Bill for free Fishing in Virginia and those Parts.

Sir *Edwin Sandys* saith, that the King divided *Virginia* into two Colonies, *viz.* the Southern Colony, and the Northern Colony; which Northern Colony was since, when a Fishing was appointed there called *New England*. . . .

Mr. Secretary saith, that *Virginia, New England, Newfoundland,* and those other foreign Parts of *America,* are not yet annexed to the Crown of *England,* but are the King's as gotten by Conquest; and therefore he thinketh it worthy the Consideration of the House, whether we shall here make Laws for the Government of those Parts; for he taketh it, that in such new Plantations the King is to govern it only by his Prerogative, and as his Majesty shall think fit: and, if in any thing he (being a Minister of the King's Prerogative) may put us in Mind of his Majesty's Prerogative, then in this. . . .

Mr. *Guy* saith, that there are divers Patents concerning the Fishing in those Parts.

Mr. *Brooke* saith, that in 11 *H.* 7 this House made a Law which tied *Ireland,* before it was annexed to this Crown; and the King's Prerogative is not touched or impeached by it, for what is here done but by the King himself; for his Majesty hath a negative Voice, so as he may refuse whether any such Bill may pass or no, though it hath before passed both Houses.

Sɪʀ *Edwin Sandys* saith, that his Majesty hath annexed to the Crown both *Virginia, New England* and *Newfoundland;* and that he knoweth *Virginia* is held as of his Majesty's Manor of *East Greenwich,* and he verily thinketh *New England* is so holden of his Majesty also. [*This Bill is committed.*][8]

DIARY OF JOHN PYM

In Defence of this Pattent was alleadged by Mr. Secretary That the abuses of the Fishermen would require some Orders For they would burne Woodes of 100 acres together. That if Regall Prerogative have power in any thinge it is in this. Newe Conquests are to be ordered by the Will of the Conquerour. Virginia is not anex't to the Crowne of England And therefore not subject to the Lawes of this Howse.

To this was Replyed. (1) The Kings Prerogative never soe magnificent as in Parliament. As yf theis partes may be Ordered by his private Graunte, much more by the Publique Graunt of the King and Kingdome. (2) Ireland, Gersy, and Garnsey are under the iurisdiccion of this Howse. The Seigniory is the Kings, but the Land is the Planters and the Trade is the Kingdomes. (3) Virginia is anexed to the Crown of England by the Tenure of East Greene-wich.[9]

AN ANONYMOUS JOURNAL

Mʀ. Sᴇᴄʀᴇᴛᴀʀʏ saith the subcommittee hath never heard the patentees, for the fishermen are wonderful unruly and the fault is on their sides not on the other. That we can make no law here for that which is a new conquest.

[8] Debate of 25 April 1621, 1 [Nicholas,] *Proceedings of 1620–21,* at 318–19.
[9] Debate of 25 April 1621, 4 *Commons Debates 1621,* at 256.

Mr. NEALE. 300 ships fish there. The places taken away, drawing them to their admiral courts. In the statute 2 Ed. 6, that fishing be to the Newfoundland.

Mr. BROOKE saith *in rebus transitoriis,* they may bind those of Virginia as those of Ireland were bound *in rebus transitoriis* not to carry wool to Calais.

To which SERJEANT ASHLEY joined in the same.

SIR EDWIN SANDYS. Virginia is holden of East Greenwich and so may be bound by the parliament.[10]

THE BELASYSE DIARY

Mr. SECRETARYE. That the Bill maye be cast out. It belonges to the kinges prerogative to governe the countries he discovers and conquers; wee are not to makes Lawes for them untill they be annexed to the Crowne of England.

BROOKE. In answere to Mr. Secretarye, the kinge indeed hath prerogative to rule, but his greatest prerogative is in parliament. If the kinge hath granted it by patente, it maye yet be examined here and repealed. The parliament hath power to binde mens persons and transitories in another kingdom. Acts of parliament here bound in Ireland till 10 H[enry] 7.

SANDES. Virginia is united alreadie in some manner to England, for Virginia doth hould of East Greenewitche by socage.[11]

NOTES OF SIR THOMAS BARRINGTON

Mr. SECRETARY. Theay doe much wrong and iniury (vizt. the fishermen doe). The Kings prerogative extends in this as

[10] Debate of 25 April 1621, 2 *Commons Debates 1621,* at 321.
[11] Debate of 25 April 1621, 5 *Commons Debates 1621,* at 98–99.

proper to his immediate government and dispose, which only is to extend to the government in those Parts newly Conquered and not as yet annext to Croune nor to be governed by any lawe but the Kings meear pleasuer who is the Conqueror. Therfor under favor I thinke the Parliament is not to discide or appoint this.

. . . .

MR. BROOKS Answer to Mr. Secretary. The King is greatest in Parliament of anywhere when the Lords and Commons aboute him; and we may make lawes, by the Kings royall assent, to bind the Kings subjects that hould of the King, and it is a different case betweene this and Se[i]g[neu]rs under government before.

SERJEANT ASHLEY. Act of Parliament is the Act of Country and th' assent of the King allso, *ergo* to goe on with the bill.[12]

The question that Thomas Hutchinson asked yet did not answer was whether the precedent of what was said and done in the commons on April 25, 1621 proved what John Adams said it proved. Had Hutchinson possessed all the various accounts that we possess today, he still might not have attempted an answer. He might have said that John Adams had not succeeded, but that was about as conclusive a statement as he could have made.

The difficulty was that Adams was using history not as history but as law and Hutchinson was looking at Adams's evidence as law not history. An historian of today, possessing only the passages of the commons that we have just read, could do little with them except summarize what was said. Mr. Secretary could be quoted as speaking about newly conquered territory being under the will of the conqueror and Virginia not being annexed to crown. To these quotations could be added the observation that "This claim was rebutted by Brooke. He pointed out that Parliament could legislate for Ireland, Jersey, and Guernsey. 'The Seigniory

[12] Debate of 25 April 1621, 3 *Commons Debates 1621*, at 82.

is the Kings, but the Land is the Planters and the Trade the Kingdomes.' "[13] The historian could then proceed to analyze these words and speculate on their meaning.

John Adams was not playing the historian's role. He was not interested in speculation. He was a lawyer seeking precedent to prove a rule of law. Had he possessed all the accounts printed above, he still might have quoted the secretary of state. He would not, however, have taken notice of Brooke or any other opposing speaker. He was interested in what was said that day not as evidence of an historical event but as authority for a constitutional dogma. The secretary's words were supposed to prove that both king and parliament understood and acted on the constitutional rule that at that time the North American colonies were not within the realm of England and, therefore, not subject to the legislature of the mother country. Had Hutchinson also possessed the records that we have today, or even had he read Nicholas or Knox, he might have quoted Brooke as evidence that everyone did not agree with the secretary, or he could have pointed out that the commons obviously disagreed with the secretary since it ignored his statement of constitutional law and enacted the bill.

Nothing would have been settled. Hutchinson's questions would have raised doubts about Adams's case; they would not have proved his own. No matter how much Hutchinson made of the fact that the commons had enacted the bill, Adams could have countered by pointing out that it had not passed the lords. Did the lords' failure to enact the bill prove that they agreed with the secretary and did not believe they had jurisdiction over the colonies? One could have made the assertion but that is all that would have been made, a not very persuasive assertion.

When John Adams introduced into the debates the evidence from 1621 he would not have cared about these questions. He was not writing history but arguing constitutional

[13] Robert Zeller, *The Parliament of 1621: A Study in Constitutional Conflict* 102 (1971).

THE REJOINDER
OF THE COUNCIL

INTRODUCTION

At the time that he was writing the replication, Thomas
Hutchinson may have realized he had no chance of accom-
plishing his original objective. It became apparent, he
wrote, "that there was no probability that either the council
or the house would recede from any point." The governor
had even given some thought to delivering his replication
and proroguing the session, but he decided it would be
inexpedient to deny "them an opportunity of being further
heard, which both council and house appeared to desire."[1]
Although he does not say so, Hutchinson may have wondered why the council bothered. What its members had to
say made little impression on him. In his replication he had
paid scant attention to the council's answer, and later, when
summarizing the debates, found little to say about the rejoinder. "The council, in their rejoinder," the governor
commented in his *History*, "attempt[ed] to explain what they
meant by the limits of the supreme authority." As far as he
could make out, the explanation was that if the " subordinate authority does not exceed its limits, and forfeit its

---

[1] 3 Hutchinson, *Massachusetts Bay*, at 272.

113

rights, but confines itself to the objects to which it was designed to extend, the supreme authority has no right to take
it away; and they say that, in fact, two such powers do subsist together, and are not incompatible." [2]

The council did say what Hutchinson said it did and said
much more besides. But because it asserted the existence of
something that the governor was convinced could not possibly exist, he was not impressed. In truth the council in its
rejoinder was caught in the same dilemma that had marred
its answer. It was, on the one hand, anxious to avoid asserting independence of the British king, while, on the other, it
rejected any suggestions of subordination to parliament. As
a result, it said little that was new. It may be suspected that
James Bowdoin was again the principal drafter, although
there is little direct evidence.

THE DOCUMENT

To this Speech [*the replication*] *His Majesty's Council on the* 25th
of February *sent to his Excellency the following Answer, by* Harrison
Gray, James Russel James Pitts, Stephen Hall, *and* James Hum-
phry, *Esq'rs; viz.*
May it please your Excellency,

As a small Part only of your Excellency's last Speech to both
Houses is addressed to the Board, there are but a few Clauses on
which we shall Remark.

With Regard to the Disorders that have arisen, your Excellency
and the Board have assigned different Causes. The Cause you
are pleased to assign, together with the Disorders themselves, we
suppose to be Effects arising from the Stamp-Act, and certain
other Acts of Parliament. If we were not mistaken in this, which
you do not assert, it so far seems to invalidate what is said in your
Speech on that Head.

We have taken Notice of this, only because it stands connected

[2] Ibid.

with another Matter, on which we would make a few further Observations. What we refer to is the general Nature of Supreme
Authority. We have already offered Reasons, in which your Excellency seems to acquiesce, to shew that, though the Term *Supreme* sometimes carries with it the idea of *unlimitted* Authority, it
cannot, in that Sense, be applied to that which is human. What is
usually denominated the Supreme Authority of a Nation must
nevertheless be limitted in it's Acts to the Objects that are properly or constitutionally cognizable by it. To illustrate our Meaning,
we beg Leave to quote a Passage from your Speech, at the Opening of this Session, where your Excellency says, "so much of the
Spirit of Liberty breathes through all Parts of the English Constitution, that although from the Nature of Government there must
be one Supreme Authority over the whole, yet this Constitution
will admit of Subordinate Powers with Legislative and Executive
Authority, greater or less, according to Local and other Circumstances."—This is very true, and implies, that the Legislative and
Executive Authority granted to the Subordinate Powers should
extend and operate as far as the Grant allows; and that, if it does
not exceed the Limits prescribed to it, and no Forfeiture be in-
curred, the Supreme Power has no rightful Authority to take
away or diminish it, or to substitute its own Acts in Cases wherein
the Acts of the Subordinate Power can, according to its Constitution, operate. To suppose the contrary is to suppose, that it has
no Property in the Privileges granted to it, for if it holds them at
the Will of the Supreme Power, which it must do by the above
Supposition, it can have no Property in them:[1] upon which Principle, which involves the Contradiction, that what is granted is in
Reality not granted, no Subordinate Power can exist. But as in
Fact the two Powers are not incompatible, and do subsist together,
each restraining its Acts to their Constitutional Objects, can we not
from hence see how the Supreme Power may supervise, regulate,
and make general Laws for the Kingdom, without interfering
with the Privileges of the Subordinate Powers within it? And also
see how it may extend its Care and Protection to its Colonies,
without injuring their Constitutional Rights?—What has been

[1] There were few other conceptualizations demonstrating how much eighteenth-
century American whigs thought like seventeenth-century English whigs, than this
argument that individual rights and privileges were not grants from government
or powers withheld from government, but "property" owned by citizens as
"birthrights".

here said concerning Supreme Authority has no Reference to the Manner in which it has been in Fact exercised, but is wholly confined to its general Nature; and if it conveys any just Idea of it, the Inferences that have been at any Time deduced from it, injurious to the Rights of the Colonists, are not well founded; and have probably arisen from a Misconception of the Nature of that Authority.

Your Excellency represents us as introducing a Number of Authorites merely to shew, that "all Taxes upon English Subjects must be levied by Virtue of the Act, not of the King alone, but in Conjunction with the Lords and Commons," and are pleased to add, that "you should very readily have allowed it; and you should as readily have allowed, that all other Acts of Legislation must be passed by the same joint Authority, and not by the King alone."— Your Excellency "would have saved us the Trouble of all those Authorities:" and on our Part we should have been as willing to have saved your Excellency the Trouble of dismembering our Argument, and from thence taking Occasion to represent it in a disadvantageous Light, or rather totally destroying it.

In Justice to ourselves it is necessary to Recapitulate that Argument adduced to prove, that the Inhabitants of this Province are not constitutionally subject to Parliamentary Taxation. In order thereto we recurred to Magna Charta and other Authorities. And the Argument abridged stands thus—That from those Authorities it appears an Essential Part of the English Constitution, "that no Tallage, or Aid, or Tax, shall be laid or levied, without the Good-will and Assent of the Freemen of the Commonalty of the Realm." That from Common Law, and the Province Charter, the Inhabitants of this Province are clearly intitled to all the Rights of free and natural Subjects within the Realm: That among those Rights must be included the essential one just mentioned concerning Aids and Taxes; and therefore that no Aids or Taxes can be levied on us constitutionally without our own Consent signified by our Representatives. From whence the Conclusion is clear, that therefore the Inhabitants of this Province are not constitutionally subject to Parliamentary Taxation.

We did not bring those Authorities to shew that Tax Acts, or any other Acts of Parliament, in order to their Validity, must have the Concurrence of the King, Lords, and Commons; but to shew, that it has been, at least from the Time of Magna Charta, an essential Right of free Subjects within the Realm, to be free from all

Taxes but such as were laid with their own Consent. And it was proper to shew this, as the Rights and Liberties, granted by the Province Charter, were to be equally extensive, to all Intents and Purposes, with those enjoyed by free and natural Subjects within the Realm. Therefore to shew our own Rights in Relation to Taxes, it was necessary to shew the Rights of Freemen within the Realm, in Relation to them: and for this Purpose those Authorities were brought, and not impertinently, as we humbly apprehend. Nor have we seen Reason to change our Sentiments with Respect to this Matter or any other contained in our Answer to your Excellency's Speech.

In the last Clause of your Speech, your Excellency informs the two Houses, "you are Authorized to say, that his Majesty will most graciously approve of every Constitutional Measure, that may contribute to the Peace, the Happiness and Prosperity of his Colony of Massachusetts Bay."—We have the highest Sense of his Majesty's Goodness in his gracious Disposition to approve of such Measures, which, as it includes his Approbation of the Constitutional Rights of his Subjects of this Colony, manifests his Inclination to protect them in those Rights; and to remove the Incroachments that have been made upon them. Of this Act of Royal Goodness they are not wholly unworthy as in Regard to Loyalty, Duty and Affection to his Majesty, they stand among the foremost of his faithful Subjects.

THE REJOINDER
OF THE HOUSE

INTRODUCTION

The leading authority on the constitutional aspects of the American Revolution described the rejoinder of the house as "one of the most remarkable in the whole series of American 'revolutionary' state papers."[1] Like the answer of the house, the rejoinder appears to be the work of John Adams. We know Samuel Adams made a contribution, as he wrote a letter to his cousin John saying he was drafting it and asking for a citation.[2] Perhaps Samuel Adams was more responsible for what was said in the rejoinder than he had been in the answer, or perhaps, as seems to have been the case before, he composed the original version. The only point that can be asserted with some certainty is that John Adams again played a role. There are several aspects of the rejoinder that bear the stamp of his legal thinking. The most notable is the paragraph attacking feudal and canon law.

Eight years earlier Adams had written "A Dissertation on

[1] Charles Howard McIlwain, *The American Revolution: a Constitutional Interpretation* 122 (1924).
[2] Letter from Samuel Adams to John Adams [February 1773], 2 Adams, *Writings*, at 430.

Canon and Feudal Law" for a lawyers' discussion club. It had been published by the *Boston Gazette* and in London and had become part of the literature of the prerevolutionary controversy.[3] The theme is summarized in the rejoinder. Just why the topic was inserted is not clear. John Adams may simply have been fond of the research and included it out of pride. A better explanation is that he was answering Hutchinson's replication. The governor had challenged his interpretation of the English constitution at the time the first colonies had been settled. Feudal law, a legal and political system in which all land is held directly or indirectly of the king, was included by Adams in the rejoinder in order to reinforce his original argument. Adams did not discuss the legal principles involved, hence it may be useful to consider something written by the proimperialist theorist William Knox. It is a simplistic yet accurate explanation of why feudalism was relevant to the issues under debate. "The right to the soil of America," Knox contended, "is allowed to have been in the Crown of England, antecedent to the settlement of any English subjects there; for the first, and all future adventurers carried with them grants from the Crown, on the lands on which they settled; and all the lands in the Colonies are at this day held by their occupiers, under titles derived from the Crown. The Crown had, therefore, a right to prescribe conditions to those who obtained those grants; and the grantees were bound, in law and equity, to a performance of those conditions."[4] Under feudalism, those conditions were known as the "tenure" by which the land was held, and the relationship between the king, the title holder, and the occupiers who held the land of him, was the link of government, the bind of allegiance, and the economic basis upon which society rested. What the rejoinder of the house claimed was that at the time the charters of Virginia and Massachusetts had been granted and the

---

[3] 1 *Papers of John Adams,* at 103–06.
[4] [William Knox,] *The Interest of the Merchants and Manufacturers of Great Britain, in the Present Contest with the Colonies Stated and Considered* 6–7 (1774).

first settlers arrived to establish the colonies, the English constitution had still been largely feudal. From that fact the legal conclusion followed that all the parties to those original grants, the king and the settlers, understood and acted on the principle that the land and, therefore, the colonies were tied to the king as feudal overlord. They were not constitutionally tied to the realm.

If we find it strange that an American whig would make arguments based on feudal legal principles, and would appeal to notions more royalist than those endorsed by contemporary British tories, we must remember that it was a constitution that was being debated. Hutchinson had insisted that the controversy was constitutional and Adams, avoiding political theory or considerations of what the constitution ought to be, was using ancient legal principles to establish what the constitution then was by delineating its antecedents. It would be well not to be misled by our own predilections. Discussions of feudal tenures and their application to current constitutional arrangements may have been more persuasive than we are able to appreciate. The weight that participants in the prerevolutionary controversy accorded to feudal concepts may be judged by considering the reaction of Arthur Lee. Writing to Samuel Adams, he went to much effort redefining and restating the argument of the house of representatives. Lee's analysis is worth considering as an indication of what a law student thought were the legal issues and the seriousness attached to doctrines that for us have lost much relevance.

Your reply to the governor's second speech is certainly unanswerable. The principle of the argument lies indeed in a very narrow compass. By the feudal law as it has been adopted into our constitution, all territory taken possession of in any manner whatsoever, by the king's subjects, rests absolutely in him. This has been the law and the practice invariably ever since we have any record of our proceedings. It is therefore that the king has ceded, given, or granted such territory to whom he pleased, and in what manner he pleased, without the intervention or consent of the state. By the state

I mean here the supreme legislature, though the word sometimes stands for the king alone; and in the debate lately in
the house of commons on General Burgoyne's motions relative to acquisitions made in India, it was admitted that the
word state, might imply the crown or the company. Taking it
however to import, as it generally does, and the governor in-
tends, the king, lords and commons, there is not a single instance in which acquired territory did rest or was conceived
to rest in them. So far from it, that the king since the last
peace made a present of the conquered and ceded lands in
the islands to the states, which was thankfully received. Which
surely would not have happened had there been an idea that
they were not his to give. Of the additional acquisitions in
America he continues to dispose at his pleasure, as absolutely
his. It is true that the king being the head of the American
states, and at the same time under the control of the two
houses of parliament here, a virtual control arises to them
from thence over his conduct in America. But this is not an
original participation of power, but an incidental and collat-
eral check over it. And certainly the mistake, or as I am more
inclined to conceive it, the sophistry of Mr. Hutchinson, consists in not distinguishing between a direct original right and
one that is merely incidental. Thus when Charles the First
became Emperor of Germany, though the states could not
claim any immediate control over his hereditary dominions,
yet previous to their gratifying him any demand, they might
have stipulated that certain things should be done in Spain,
and then they would virtually govern that country. It seems
to me that this is the only method by which a British parliament can constitutionally interfere in the government of the
colonies. But certainly this is a great question, and one which
this country will never concede to reason. Necessity alone will
prevail with her to give up this claim, however repugnant to
constitutional principles.[5]

That young Arthur Lee, writing a private letter to the
already persuaded Samuel Adams, would take so much
time and trouble to reinforce and expand the rejoinder's

[5] Letter from Arthur Lee to Samuel Adams, 11 June 1773, in 1 Lee, *Arthur Lee,*
at 230–31.

discussion of feudal law deserves consideration. Doubts about the accuracy of his law need not concern us. Lee thought the discussion persuasive and he believed Adams would as well.

There is one other part of the rejoinder that certainly owes something to John Adams.[6] It appears near the end of the document where a lawyer's distinction is drawn. The house was dealing with one of the most difficult historical facts with which American whigs had to contend: that the colonies in 1689 had universally acknowledged the constitutionality of the election by parliament of William and Mary as the king and queen of England. In restrospect that election marks the emergence of parliament's supremacy. By removing James II and proclaiming other monarchs in his place, the commons and lords had established their primacy. If they could name the king, then they were superior to him. More to the point, parliament had acted alone. It had not felt a constitutional obligation "to call for the advice and assistance of the dependent states."[7]

Thomas Hutchinson had avoided the topic of the Glorious Revolution in his original address. In the replication he had referred to it cautiously, seeking to demonstrate that the Massachusetts assembly had acknowledged parliament's supremacy by obeying certain statutes, such as one imposing an oath of allegiance to William and Mary. He seems to have been saying that Massachusetts acquiesced in the new constitutional arrangement, but he did not do so by insisting that parliament had made itself sovereign and there was nothing Americans could do except obey. Instead he stressed what American whigs themselves stressed, the royal connection, and asked how they had managed to obtain William and Mary in place of James II yet avoided the authority that had ordained the succession. "If," he asked, "you should disown that Authority which has Power even to

---

[6] Joseph Hawley apparently was not in Boston at the time and did not contribute to the rejoinder.

[7] [Phelps,] *Rights of the Colonies*, at 17–18.

change the Succession to the Crown, are you in no Danger of denying the Authority of our most gracious Sovereign, which I am sure none of you have in your Thoughts?"

The most notable feature of Hutchinson's handling of the Glorious Revolution was his caution. He did not claim all that he might have, certainly not as much as did Thomas Pownall when he said parliament had assumed sovereignty and the colonies were unilaterally bound. One reason previously noted is that Hutchinson hoped to avoid issues of consent and representation. Another explanation is that the governor did not want to be confronted with yet a third question, one perhaps more difficult to answer than how the colonies had consented to parliamentary supremacy or why they were not represented at Westminster. If by acquiescence or adoption the Americans were bound by the consequences of the Glorious Revolution, why did they not enjoy its benefits? An example was judicial tenure for life rather than at the pleasure of the crown, a constitutional innovation that made the bench somewhat independent of politics in Great Britain and had not been extended to America. If the colonies were bound to the Glorious Revolution doctrine of parliamentary supremacy but not the Glorious Revolution doctrine of judicial tenure *quamdiu se bene gesserint,* they were not being treated equally with their fellow subjects at home.

Hutchinson understood the issue. He rejected the argument that the colonies were constitutionally entitled to judges serving at good behavior rather than pleasure,[8] and that rejection may explain why he did not discuss the relationship between the Glorious Revolution and America's subjection to parliamentary supremacy. The house of representatives did take up the question, admitting that the citizens of Massachusetts Bay had, by the implication of their actions, consented to the elevation of William and Mary to the throne. That consent was limited to the crown. It did

---

[8] "There has been a change in the constitution of England in respect of the tenure of the office of the Judges. How does this give a claim to America?" [Hutchinson,] *Strictures Upon the Declaration,* at 18.

not include, and could not be read to include, consent to the doctrine of parliamentary supremacy.[9] In his surrejoinder Hutchinson discussed neither the argument nor the statutory evidence the house offered to document that argument.

THE DOCUMENT

And on Tuesday March *2d, Mr.* Hancock, *Mr.* Gorham, *Major* Fuller, *Capt.* Greenleafe, *Capt.* Heath, *Mr.* Phillips, *Capt.* Nye, *Capt.* Brown *of* Watertown, *and Capt.* Gardner, *a Committee of the House of Representatives, waited on the Governor with their Answer as follows,*[1] *Viz.*

May it please your Excellency,

In your Speech at the Opening of the present Session, your Excellency express'd your Displeasure at some late Proceedings of the Town of Boston, and other principal Towns in the Province. And in another Speech to both Houses we have your repeated Exceptions at the same Proceedings as being "unwarrantable," and of a dangerous Nature and Tendency; "against which you thought yourself bound to call upon us to join with you in bearing a proper Testimony." This House have not discovered any Principles advanced by the Town of Boston, that are unwarrantable by the Constitution; nor does it appear to us that they have "invited every other Town and District in the Province to adopt their Principles." We are fully convinced that it is our Duty to bear our Testimony against "Innovations of a dangerous Nature and

---

[9] Edward Bancroft, offering historical evidence to prove a closely related constitutional result, observed that in January 1659, Virginia proclaimed " 'Charles the Second, King of *England, Scotland, France, Ireland,* and VIRGINIA,' some time before his Restoration to *England.*" [Bancroft,] *Remarks,* at 52.

[1] The house ordered Hutchinson's speech read at least four times before appointing a committee of reply made up of the same members as before except that Hawley was replaced by Thomas Denny. Sessions for 16, 17, 18 February 1773, *Journal of the House,* at 243–45. The draft of the rejoinder was twice read to the house before it was accepted by voice vote and sent to the governor. Session for 2 March 1773, *ibid.,* at 267—68. The rejoinder is printed in *ibid.,* at 268–80.

Tendency:" But is clearly our Opinion, that it is the indisputable Right of all or any of his Majesty's Subjects in this Province, regularly and orderly to meet together to state the Grievances they labor under; and to propose and unite in such constitutional Measures as they shall judge necessary or proper to obtain Redress. This Right has been frequently exercised by his Majesty's Subjects within the Realm; and we do not recollect an Instance, since the happy Revolution, when the two Houses of Parliament have been called upon to discountenance or bear their Testimony against it, in a Speech from the Throne.

Your Excellency is pleased to take Notice of some things which we "alledge" in our Answer to your first Speech; and the Observation you make, we must confess, is as natural and as undeniably true, as any one that could have been made, that "if our Foundation shall fail us *in every Part of it,* the Fabrick we have rais'd upon it, must certainly fall." You think, this Foundation will fail us; but we wish your Excellency had condescended to a Consideration of what we have "adduced in Support of our Principles." We might then perhaps have had some things offered for our Conviction, more than bare Affirmations; which, we must beg to be excused if we say, are far from being sufficient, though they came with your Excellency's Authority, for which however we have a due Regard.

Your Excellency says that "as English Subjects and agreeable to the Doctrine of the Feudal Tenure all our Lands are held mediately or immediately of the Crown." We trust your Excellency does not mean to introduce the Feudal system in it's Perfection; which to use the Words of one of our greatest Historians, was "a State of perpetual War, Anarchy and Confusion; calculated solely for Defence against the Assaults of any foreign Power, but in it's Provision for the interior Order and Tranquility of Society extremely defective."[2] "A Constitution so contradictory to all the Principles that govern Mankind, could never be brought about

[2] It is said this sentence is a composite of phrases taken from one author. 1 *Papers of John Adams,* at 345n1. "But though the Feudal policy seems to be so admirably calculated for defense against the assaults of any foreign power, its provisions for the interior order and tranquility of society were extremely defective." 1 William Robertson, *The History of the Reign of the Emperor Charles V. With a View of the Progress of Society in Europe, From the Subversion of the Roman Empire, to the Beginning of the Sixteenth Century* 15 (1769).

but by foreign Conquest or native Usurpation:"[3] And a very celebrated Writer calls it "that most iniquitous and absurd Form of Government by which human Nature was so shamefully degraded."[4] This System of Iniquity by a strange Kind of Fatality, "though originally form'd for an Encampment and for Military Purposes only, spread over a great Part of Europe:" and to serve the Purposes of Oppression and Tyranny "was adopted by Princes and wrought into their Civil Constitutions;"[5] and aided by the Canon Law, calculated by the Roman Pontiff, to exalt himself above all that is called God, it prevailed to the almost utter Extinction of Knowledge, Virtue, Religion and Liberty from that Part of the Earth. But from the Time of the Reformation, in Proportion as Knowledge, which then darted its Rays upon the benighted World, increas'd and spread among the People, they grew impatient under this heavy Yoke: And the most virtuous and sensible among them, to whose Steadfastness we in this distant Age and Climate are greatly indebted, were determined to get rid of it: And tho' they have in a great Measure subdued it's Power and Influence in England, they have never yet totally eradicated its Principles.[6]

Upon these Principles the King claimed an absolute Right to and a perfect Estate in all the Lands within his Dominions; but how he came by this absolute Right and perfect Estate is a Mystery which we have never seen unravelled, nor is it our Business or Design at present to enquire. He granted Parts or Parcels of it to his Friends the Great Men, and they granted lesser Parcels to

[3] Henry Home, Lord Kames, *Essays Upon Several Subjects Concerning British Antiquities* 1–2 (3d ed. 1763).

[4] J. J. Rousseau, *A Treatise on the Social Compact: Or the Principles of Politic Law* 164 (1764).

[5] "[F]or the same purposes of tyranny, cruelty and lust, which had dictated the *canon* law, it [feudal law] was soon adopted by almost all the Princes of Europe, and wrought into the constitutions of their government. —It was originally a code of laws, for a vast army in a perpetual encampment." [Adams,] "Dissertation on Canon and Feudal Law," at 115.

[6] John Adams associated canon law with feudal law on the theory that they were "the two greatest systems of tyranny" to spring up since "the promulgation of Christianity." Their power over people was destroyed in England by the spread of education. "[W]herever a general knowledge and sensibility have prevailed among the people, arbitrary government and every kind of oppression have lessened and disappeared in proportion," [Adams,] "Dissertation on Canon and Feudal Law," at 112–13.

their Tenants: All therefore derived their Right and held their Lands, upon these Principles, mediately or immediately of the King; which Mr. *Blackstone* however calls "in Reality a meer Fiction of our English Tenures."[7]

By what Right in Nature and Reason the Christian Princes in Europe claimed the Lands of Heathen People, upon a Discovery made by any of their Subjects, is equally mysterious: Such however was the Doctrine universally prevailing when the Lands in America were discovered; but as the People of England upon those Principles held all the Lands they possessed by Grants from the King, and the King had never granted the Lands in America *to them,* it is certain they could have no Sort of Claim to them: Upon the Principles advanced, the Lordship and Dominion like that of the Lands in England, was in the King solely: and a Right from thence accrued to him of disposing such Territories under such Tenure and for such Services to be performed, as the King or Lord thought proper. But how the Grantees *became* Subjects of England, that is the Supreme Authority of the Parliament, your Excellency has not explained to us. We conceive that upon the Feudal Principles all Power is in the King; they afford us no Idea *of Parliament.* "The Lord was in early Times the Legislator and Judge over all his Feudatories," says Judge Blackstone.[8] By the Struggles for Liberty in England from the Days of King John to the last happy Revolution, the Constitution has been gradually changing for the better;[9] and upon the more rational Principles that all Men by Nature are in a State of Equality in Respect of Jurisdiction and Dominion, Power in England has been more equally divided. And thus also in America, though we hold our Lands agreeably to the Feudal Principles of the King; yet our Predecessors wisely took care to enter into Compact with the King that Power here should also be equally divided agreeable to the original fundamental Principles of the English Constitution, de-

---

[7] "[I]t became a fundamental maxim and necessary principle (though in reality a mere fiction) of our English tenures, 'that the king is the universal lord and original proprietor of all the lands in his kingdom; and that no man doth or can possess any part of it, but what has mediately or immediately been derived as a gift from him, to be held upon feudal services.' " 2 Blackstone, *Commentaries,* at 51.

[8] Ibid., at 54.

[9] This statement practically stands alone in the entire debate as an indication that at least one of the parties did not regard the British constitution as a static, changeless system of government.

clared in Magna Charter, and other Laws and Statutes of England, made to confirm them.

Your Excellency says, "you can by no Means concede to us that it is now or was when the Plantations were first granted the Prerogative of the Kings of England to constitute a Number of new Governments altogether independent of the Sovereign Authority of the English Empire." By the Feudal Principles upon which you say "all the Grants which have been made of America are founded" "the Constitutions of the Emperor have the Force of Law." If our Government be considered as merely Feudatory, we are subject to the King's absolute Will, and there is no Room for the Authority of Parliament, as the Sovereign Authority of the British Empire. Upon these Principles, what could hinder the King's constituting a Number of independent Governments in America? That King Charles the First did actually set up a Government in this Colony, conceding to it Powers of making and executing Laws, without any Reservation to the English Parliament, of Authority to make future Laws binding therein, is a Fact which your Excellency has not disproved if you have denied it. Nor have you shewn that the Parliament or Nation objected to it, from whence we have inferred that it was an acknowledged Right. And we cannot conceive, why the King has not the same Right to alienate and dispose of Countries acquired by the Discovery of his Subjects, as he has to "restore upon a Treaty of Peace Countries which have been acquired in War," carried on at the Charge of the Nation; or to "sell and deliver up any Part of his Dominions to a foreign Prince or State, against the General Sense of the Nation" which is "an Act of Power" or Prerogative which your Excellency allows.[10] You tell us that "when any New Countries are

[10] This argument indicates that despite what was said in the previous paragraph, the constitution of seventeenth-century England (when the colonies were created by grant of the crown) was equated with the constitution of eighteenth-century Great Britain (in which the crown's prerogative powers were greatly curtailed). The house defended its interpretation of the constitution by an analogy to powers the king (in theory) still possessed, rather than by considering what powers, since abrogated, the crown had possessed before the Glorious Revolution of 1688 and the advent of parliamentary supremacy. Hutchinson was neither convinced nor impressed. "A right in the crown to dispose of America, could not be inferred from its prerogative of restoring countries acquired in war upon a treaty of peace, the prerogative of making war and peace being in the crown, this power of restoring countries acquired was incidental and necessary—and it discovered [revealed] a want of candour, to suppose when he [Hutchinson] spoke of an act, or a mee'r

discovered by English Subjects, according to the general Law and Usage of Nations, *they become Part of the State."* The Law of Nations is or ought to be founded on the Law of Reason. It was the Saying of Sir Edwin Sandis, in the great Case of the Union of the Realm of Scotland with England, which is applicable to our present Purpose, that "there being no Precedent for this Case in the Law, the Law is deficient; and the Law being deficient, Recourse is to be had to Custom; and Custom being insufficient, we must recur to natural Reason," the greatest of all Authorities, which he adds "is the Law of Nations."[11] The Opinions therefore, and Determinations of the greatest Sages and Judges of the Law in the Exchequer Chamber ought not to be considered as decisive or binding in our present Controversy with your Excellency, any further than they are consonant to *natural Reason.*[12] If however we were to recur to such Opinions and Determinations we should find very great Authorities in our Favour, to show that the Statutes of England are not binding on those who are not represented in Parliament there. The Opinion of Lord Coke that Ireland was bound by Statutes of England wherein they *were named,* if compared with his other Writings, appears manifestly to be grounded upon a Supposition, that Ireland had by an Act of their own, in the Reign of King John, consented to be thus bound, and upon any other Supposition this Opinion would be against *Reason;* for *Consent only* gives human Laws their Force. We beg Leave, upon what your Excellency has observed of the Colony becoming a Part of the State, to subjoin the Opinions of several learned Civilians, as quoted by a very able Lawyer in this Country;[13] "Colonies," says Puffendorf [*sic*], "are settled in different Methods. For either the Colony *continues* a *Part* of the Common Wealth it was sent out from; or else is obliged to pay a dutiful Regard to the Mother Common Wealth, and to be in Readiness to defend and vindicate its Honor, and so is united by a Sort of unequal Confederacy; or lastly, is *erected into a separate Common Wealth* and *assumes the same*

---

act, of *power* in selling any part of the dominions to a foreign prince, that he intended the crown had a *just prerogative* to make such sale." [Hutchinson,] "Additions," at 58–59.

[11] Le Case de Union del Realm, d'Escose, *ove* Angleterre, Moore, *Cases,* at 791.

[12] Too much should not be made of this argument. Although the house for the first time refers to natural reason, it does so on the authority of the court of exchequer chamber and, therefore, is making an argument based on English law.

[13] James Otis. See Otis, *Rights,* at 26–27.

Rights, with the State it descended from."[14] And King Tullius, as quoted by the same learned Author from Grotius, says "We look upon it to be neither Truth nor Justice that Mother Cities ought of Necessity and *by the Law of Nature* to *rule over the Colonies.*"[15]

Your Excellency has misinterpreted what we have said, "that no Country by the Common Law, was subject to the Laws or the Parliament but the Realm of England," and are pleased to tell us that we have expressed ourselves "*Incautiously.*" We beg Leave to recite the Words of the Judges of England in the beforementioned Case to our Purpose. "If a King go out of England with a Company of his Servants, Allegiance remaineth among his Subjects and Servants, altho' he be out of his Realm *whereto his Laws are confined.*"[16] We did not mean to say, as your Excellency would suppose, that "the Common Law prescribes Limits to the Extent of the Legislative Power," though we shall always affirm it to be true of the Law of Reason and natural Equity. Your Excellency thinks you have made it appear, that the Colony of Massachusetts-Bay is holden as feudatory of the Imperial Crown of England;" and therefore you say, "to use the Words of a very great Authority in a Case in *some Respects* analogous to it," being feudatory it necessarily follows, that it is under the Government of the King's Laws." Your Excellency has not named this Authority; but we conceive his Meaning must be, that being Feudatory, it is under the Government of the King's Laws *absolutely;* for as we have before said the Feudal System admits of no Idea of the Authority of Parliament, and this would have been the Case of the Colony but for the Compact with the King in the Charter.

Your Excellency says, that "Persons thus holding *under the Crown* of England remain or *become* Subjects of England;" by which we suppose your Excellency to mean, subject to the Supreme Authority of Parliament "to all Intents and Purposes as fully as if any of the Royal Manors, &c. within the Realm had been Granted to them upon the like Tenure." We apprehend with Submission, your Excellency is Mistaken in supposing that our Allegiance is due to the Crown of England. Every Man swears Allegiance for himself to his own King in his Natural Person.

[14] Pufendorf, *Law of Nature,* at 125 [Book VIII, Chap. 11, Sec. 6].

[15] 2 Grotius, *Rights of War,* at 224 [Book II, Chap. 9, Sec. 10]. The term "Mother Cities" comes from Otis. Grotius said "Metropolis's" ought not rule over colonies. Otis, *Rights,* at 26.

[16] Le Case de Union, del Realm, d'Escose, *ove* Angleterre, Moore, *Cases,* at 798.

"Every Subject is presumed by Law to be Sworn to the King, which is to his Natural Person," says Lord Coke. *Rep. on Calvins Case.* "The Allegiance is due to his Natural Body."[17] And he says "in the Reign of Edward II. the Spencers, the Father and the Son, to cover the Treason hatched in their Hearts, invented this damnable and damned Opinion, that *Homage* and Oath of Allegiance was more by Reason of the King's Crown, that is of his politick Capacity, than by Reason of the Person of the King; upon which Opinion they infer'd execrable and detestable Consequents."[18] The Judges of England, all but one, in the Case of the Union between Scotland and England, declared that "Allegiance followeth the natural Person not the politick;"[19] and "to prove the Allegiance to be tied to the Body natural of the King, and not to the Body politick, the Lord Coke cited the Phrases of diverse Statutes, mentioning our *natural* liege Sovereign."[20]—If then the Homage and Allegiance is not to the Body politick of the King, then it is not to him as the Head or any Part of that Legislative Authority, which your Excellency says "is equally extensive with the Authority of the Crown throughout every Part of the Dominion;" and your Excellency's Observations thereupon must fail. The same Judges mention the Allegiance of a Subject to the Kings of England who is out of the Reach and Extent of the Laws of England;[21] which is perfectly reconcileable with the Principles of our

---

[17] "Ligeance is due only to the King; . . . It is true, that the King hath two Capacities in him: One a natural Body, being descended of the Blood Royal of the Realm; and this Body is of the creation of Almighty God, and is subject to death, infirmity, and such like: The other is a politick Body or Capacity, so called, because it is framed by the policy of Man . . . and in this capacity the King is esteemed to be Immortal, Invisible, not subject to Death, Infirmity, Infancy, Nonage, &c. . . . . Now se[e]ing the King hath but one Person, and several Capacities, and one politick Capacity for the Realm of England, and another for the Realm of Scotland, it is necessary to be considered, to which Capacity ligeancy is due. And it was resolved, that it was due to the natural person of the King (which is ever accompanied with the politick capacity, and the politick capacity as it were appropriated to the Natural capacity,) and is not due to the politik capacity only, that is, to his Crown or Kingdom distinct from his natural capacity, and that for diverse Reasons. First, every Subject . . . is presumed by Law to be sworn to the King, which is to his natural person . . . ." *Calvin's Case,* at 11. See also, Calvin's Case, *Coke's Reports,* 1, 10 (1609).

[18] *Calvin's Case,* at 12.

[19] Le Case del Union, del Realm, d'Escose, *ove* Angleterre, Moore, *Cases,* at 798.

[20] Ibid., at 799.

[21] "King *Ed. I.* went in Person into *France,* to a Marriage; one of his servants in *France* stole two silver dishes, for which he was apprehended by the *French;* the

Ancestors quoted before from your Excellency's History, but upon your Excellency's Principles appears to us to be an Absurdity. The Judges, speaking of a Subject, say, "although his Birth was out of the Bounds of the Kingdom of England, and *out of the Reach and Extent of the Laws of England,* yet if it were *within the Allegiance of the King of England,* &c. Normandy, Acquitain, Gascoign, and other Places within the Limits of France, and consequently out of the Realm or Bounds of the Kingdom of England, were in Subjection to the Kings of England."[22] And the Judges say, *"Rex et Regnum* be not so Relatives, as a King can be King but of one Kingdom, which clearly holdeth not but that his Kingly Power extending to divers Nations and Kingdoms, all owe him equal Subjection and are equally born to the Benefit of his Protection, and altho' he is to govern them *by their distinct Laws,* yet any one of the People coming into the other is to have the Benefit of the Laws wheresoever he cometh."[23] So they are not to be deemed Aliens, as your Excellency in your Speech supposes in any of the Dominions; all which accords with the Principles our Ancestors held. "And he is to bear the Burden of Taxes of the *Place where he cometh,* but living in one or for his Livelihood in one, *he is not to be taxed in the other,* because Laws ordain Taxes, Impositions and Charges as a Discipline of Subjection particularized to every particular Nation:"[24] Nothing we think, can be more clear to our Purpose than this Decision, of Judges, perhaps as learned as ever adorned the English Nation; or in Favor of America in her present Controversy with the Mother State.

Your Excellency says, that by our not "distinguishing between the Crown of England and the Kings and Queens of England in their personal or natural Capacities, we have been led into a fundamental Error." Upon this very Distinction we have availed our-

---

King required to have him redelivered being his subject and of his Train; and upon dispute in the Parliament of *Paris,* he was sent to the King of *England* to do his justice upon him, whereupon he was tryed before the Steward and Marshal of the Kings house, and executed in *France.* . . . Which proveth that the King's law followeth his Allegiance out of the local limit of the Laws of *England.*" Ibid., at 798–99.

[22] The quotation is legally though not literally correct. The judges said that if the birth occurred outside England, "yet if it were within the allegiance of the Kings of *England,* the King was not to have his Escheat as an-alien, as at this time diverse places that were within the limits of *France,* were in subjection to the Kings of England." Ibid., at 800.

[23] Ibid., at 805.

[24] Ibid., at 805.

selves. We have said that our Ancestors considered the Land which they took Possession of in America as out of the Bounds of the Kingdom of England, and out of the Reach and Extent of the Laws of England; and that the King also even in the Act of grant-ing the Charter, considered the Territory as *not within* the Realm; that the King had an absolute Right in himself to dispose of the Lands, and that this was not disputed by the Nation; nor could the Lands on any solid Grounds be claimed by the Nation, and therefore our Ancestors received the Lands by Grant from the King, and at the same Time compacted with him and promised him Homage and Allegiance, not in his publick or politick but nat-ural Capacity only. If it be difficult for us to show how the King acquired a Title to this Country in his natural Capacity, or sepa-rate from his Relation to his Subjects, which we confess, yet we conceive it will be equally difficult for your Excellency to show how the Body Politick and Nation of England acquired it. Our Ancestors supposed it was acquired by neither; and therefore they declared, as we have before quoted from your History, that saving their actual Purchase from the Natives, of the Soil, the Dominion, the Lordship, and Sovereignty, they had in the Sight of God and Man, no Right and Title to what they possessed. How much clearer then in natural Reason and Equity must our Title be, who hold Estates dearly purchased at the Expence of our own as well as our Ancestors Labour, and defended by them with Treasure and Blood.

Your Excellency has been pleased to confirm, rather than deny or confute a Piece of History which you say we took from an anonimous Pamphlet, and by which you "fear we have been too easily misled." It may be gathered from your own Declaration and other Authorities besides the anonimous Pamphlet, that the House of Commons took Exception, not at the King's having made an absolute Grant of the Territory, but at the Claim of an exclusive Right to the Fishery on the banks and Sea Coast, by Virtue of the Patent. At this you say "the House of Commons was alarmed, and a Bill was brought in for allowing a free Fishery." And upon this Occasion your Excellency allows, that "one of the Secretaries of State declared that the Plantations were not an-nexed to the Crown, and so were not within the Jurisdiction of Parliament." If we should concede to what your Excellency sup-poses might possibly or "perhaps" be the Case, that the Secretary made this Declaration "as his own Opinion," the Event showed that it was the Opinion of the King too; for it is not to be accounted for upon any other Principle, that he would have denied his Royal Assent to a Bill formed for no other Purpose, but to grant his Subjects in England the Privilege of Fishing on the Sea Coasts in America.[25] The Account published by Sir Ferdinando Gorges himself, of the Proceedings of Parliament *on this Occasion,* your Excellency thinks will remove all Doubt of the Sense of the Nation and of the Patentees of this Patent or Charter in 1620. "This Narrative, you say, has all the Appearance of Truth and Sincerity," which we do not deny: And to us it carries this Conviction with it, that "what was objected" in Parliament was, the exclusive Claim of Fishing only. His imagining that he had satisfied the House after divers Attendances, that the Planting a Colony was of much more Consequence than a *simple disorderly Course of Fishing,* is sufficient for our Conviction. We know that the Nation was at that Time alarmed with Apprehensions of Monopolies;[26] and if the Patent of New-England was presented by the two Houses as a Grievance, it did not show, as your Excellency supposes, "the Sense they then had of their Authority over this new-acquired Territory," but only their Sense of the Grievance of a Monopoly of the Sea.

We are happy to hear your Excellency say, that "our Remarks upon and Construction of the Words *not repugnant to the Laws of England,* are much the same with those of Council." It serves to confirm us in our Opinion, in what we take to be the most important Matter of Difference between your Excellency and the two Houses. After saying, that the Statute of 7th and 8th of William and Mary favors the Construction of the Words as intending such Laws of England as are made more immediately to respect us, you tell us, that "the Province Agent Mr. Drummer in his much applauded Defence, says that *then* a Law of the Plantations may

---

[25] The house seems to have compounded two arguments. It referred to the fishery bill in the session of 1621, and asked whether the objection raised to it by the secretary of state was also an objection stated by James I. It was, however, King Charles, not King James, who earlier was said to reject the bill. In this sentence the implication was that King James denied the royal assent.

[26] Monopolies were one of the chief constitutional grievances that year. For a discussion see Elizabeth Read Foster, "The Procedure of the House of Commons against Patents and Monopolies, 1621–1624," in *Conflict in Stuart England: Essays in Honour of Wallace Notestein* 59–85 (William Appleton Aiken and Basil Duke Henning ed., 1960).

be said to be repugnant to a Law made in Great-Britain, when it flatly contradicts it so far as the Law made there mentions and relates to the Plantations." This is plain and obvious to common Sense, and therefore cannot be denied. But if your Excellency will read a Page or two further in that excellent Defence, you will see that he mentions this as the Sense of the Phrase, as taken from an Act of Parliament,[27] rather than as the Sense he would chuse himself to put upon it; and he expressly designs to shew, in Vindication of the Charter, that in that Sense of the Words, there never was a Law made in the Plantations repugnant to the Laws of Great-Britain. He gives another Construction much more likely to be the true Intent of the Words; namely, "that the Patentees shall not presume under Colour of their particular Charters to make any Laws *inconsistent with the Great Charter and other Laws of England, by which the Lives, Liberties, and Properties of Englishmen are secured.*"[28] This is the Sense in which our Ancestors understood the Words; and therefore they were unwilling to conform to the Acts of Trade, and disregarded them till they made Provision to give them Force in the Colony by a Law of their own; saying that "the Laws of England did not reach America: And those Acts were an Invasion of their Rights, Liberties, and Properties," because they were not "represented in Parliament." The Right of being governed only by Laws which were made by Persons in whose Election they had a Voice, they looked upon as the Foundation of English Liberties. By the Compact with the King in the Charter, they were to be as free in America, as they would have been if they had remained within the Realm; and therefore they freely asserted that they "were to be governed by Laws made by themselves and by Officers chosen by themselves." Mr. Drummer says, "It seems reasonable enough to think that the Crown," and he might have added our Ancestors, "intended by this Injunction to provide for all its Subjects, that they might not be oppressed by

---

[27] "That all Law, By-Laws, Usages, or Customs at this Time, or which hereafter shall be in Practice, or endeavoured or pretended to be in Force or Practice in any of the Plantations, which are in any wise repugnant to the before mentioned Laws or any of them, so for as they do relate to the said Plantations, or any of them, or which are any ways repugnant to this present Act, or any other Law hereafter to be made in this Kingdom, so far as such Law shall relate to and mention the said Plantations, are illegal, null, and void, to all Intents and Purposes whatsoever." 7&8 William III, cap. 22, sec. 9.

[28] Dummer, *Defence of the Charters,* at 31.

Arbitrary Power—but—being still Subjects, they should be protected by the same mild Laws and enjoy the same happy Government as if they continued within the Realm."[29] And considering the Words of the Charter in this Light, he looks upon them as designed to be a Fence against Oppression and despotic Power. But the Construction which your Excellency puts upon the Words, reduces us to a State of Vassallage, and exposes us to Oppression and despotic Power, whenever a Parliament shall see fit to make Laws for that Purpose and put them in Execution.

We flatter ourselves that from the large Extracts we have made from your Excellency's History of the Colony,[30] it appears evidently, that under both Charters it hath been the Sense of the People and of the Government that they were not under the Jurisdiction of Parliament. We pray you again to recur to those Quotations and our Observations upon them: And we wish to have your Excellency's judicious Remarks. When we adduced that History to prove that the Sentiments of *private* persons of Influence, four or five Years after the Restoration, were very different from what your Excellency apprehended them to be when you delivered your Speech, you seem to concede to it by telling us "it was, as you take it, from the *Principles imbibed* in those Times of Anarchy (preceeding the Restoration) that they disputed the Authority of Parliament;" but you add, "the Government would not venture to dispute it." We find in the same History a Quotation from a Letter of Mr. *Stoughton,* dated 17 Years after the Restoration, mentioning "the Country's not taking Notice of the Acts of Navigation *to observe them.*"[31] And it was, as we take it, after that

[29] Dummer, *Defence of the Charters,* at 31–32.

[30] That the extracts were large might be disputed by historians who insist the whig constitutional argument was not sincere, but a screen for economic or nationalistic motivations. Samuel Eliot Morison pointed out that "Hutchinson's *History of Massachusetts Bay* containing a full and accurate account of the 'Free-State' attitude of the Bay Colony, appeared in 1764. If the Massachusetts leaders of the 1770's had felt that they were defending traditional local liberties, they would have used this material and flung quotations from Hutchinson in his own face. They never did." Morison, "Remarks," at 64.

[31] Stoughton's full sentence reads: "The country's not taking notice of these acts of navigation to observe them, hath been the most unhappy neglect that we could have fallen into, for, more and more every day, we find it most certain, that without a fair compliance in that matter, there can be nothing expected but a total breach, and the storms of displeasure that may be." 1 Hutchinson, *Massachusetts Bay,* at 270.

Time, that the Government declared in a Letter to their Agents, that they had not submitted to them; and they ventured to "dispute" the Jurisdiction, asserting that they apprehended the Acts to be an Invasion of the Rights, Liberties and Properties of the Subjects of his Majesty in the Colony, *they not being represented in Parliament;* and that "the Laws of England *did not reach America.*"[32] It very little avails in Proof that they conceded to the Supreme Authority of Parliament, their telling the Commissioners "that the Act of Navigation had for some Years before been observed here, that they knew not of its being greatly violated, and that such Laws as appeared to be against it were repealed." It may as truly be said now, that the Revenue Acts are observed by some of the People of this Province; but it cannot be said that the Government and People of this Province have conceded that the Parliament had Authority to make such Acts to be observed here. Neither does their Declarations to the Commissioners that such Laws as appeared to be against the Act of Navigation were repealed, prove their Concession of the Authority of Parliament, by any means so much as their making Provision for giving Force to an Act of Parliament within this Province, by a deliberate and solemn Act or Law of their own, proves the contrary.

You tell us, that "the Government four or five Years before the Charter was vacated more explicitly," that is than by a Conversation with the Commissioners, "acknowledged the Authority of Parliament, and voted that their Governor should take the Oath required of him faithfully to do and perform all Matters and Things enjoined by the Acts of Trade." But does this, may it please your Excellency, show their explicit Acknowledgment of the Authority of Parliament? Does it not rather show directly the contrary: For, what need could there be for their Vote or Authority to require him to take the Oath already required of him by the Act of Parliament, unless both he and they judged that an Act of Parliament was not of Force sufficient to bind him to take such Oath? We do not deny, but on the contrary are fully persuaded that your Excellency's Principles in Government are still of the same with what they appear to be in the History; for you there say, that "the passing this Law plainly shows the wrong Sense they had of the Relation they stood in to England."[33] But

---

[32] Ibid., at 272 (quotations cited in the answer of the house).
[33] 1 Hutchinson, *Massachusetts Bay,* at 272.

we are from hence convinced that your Excellency when you wrote the History was of our Mind in this Respect, that our Ancestors in passing the Law discovered their Opinion that they were without the Jurisdiction of Parliament: For it was upon this Principle alone that they shewed the wrong Sense they had in your Excellency's Opinion, of the Relation they stood in to England.

Your Excellency in your second Speech condescends to point out to us the Acts and Doings of the General Assembly which relates to Acts of Parliament, which you think "demonstrates that they have been acknowledged by the Assembly or submitted to by the People:" Neither of which in our Opinion shows that it was the Sense of the Nation, and our Predecessors when they first took Possession of this Plantation or Colony by a Grant and Charter from the Crown, that they were to remain subject to the Supreme Authority of the English Parliament.

Your Excellency seems chiefly to rely upon our Ancestors, after the Revolution "proclaiming King William and Queen Mary in the Room of King James," and taking the Oaths to them, "the Alteration of the Form of Oaths from Time to Time," and finally "the Establishment of the Form which every one of us has complied with, as the Charter in express Terms requires and makes our Duty." We do not know that it has ever been a Point in Dispute whether the Kings of England were ipso facto Kings in and over this Colony or Province. The Compact was made between King Charles the First, his Heirs and Successors, and the Governor and Company, their Heirs and Successors. It is easy upon this Principle to account for the Acknowledgment of and Submission to King William and Queen Mary as Successors of Charles the First, in the Room of King James: Besides it is to be considered, that the People in the Colony as well as in England had suffered under the TYRANT James, by which he had alike forfeited his Right to reign over both. There had been a Revolution here as well as in England. The Eyes of the People here were upon William and Mary, and the News of their being proclaimed in England was as your Excellency's History tells us, "the most joyful News ever received in New-England."[34] And if they were not proclaimed here "by virtue of an Act of the Colony," it was, as we think may be concluded from the Tenor of your History, with the

[34] Ibid., at 328.

general or universal Consent of the People as apparently as if "such Act had passed." It is *Consent alone,* that makes any human Laws binding; and as a learned Author observes, a purely *voluntary* Submission to an Act, because it is highly in our Favor and for our Benefit, is in all Equity and Justice to be deemed as not at all proceeding from the *Right* we include in the Legislators, that they thereby obtain an *Authority* over us, and that ever hereafter we must obey them of *Duty.* We would observe that one of the first Acts of the General Assembly of this Province since the present Charter, was an Act requiring the taking the Oaths mentioned in an Act of Parliament, to which you refer us: For what Purpose was this Act of the Assembly passed, if it was the Sense of the Legislators that the Act of Parliament was in Force in the Province. And at the same Time another Act was made for the Establishment of other Oaths necessary to be taken; both which Acts have the Royal Sanction, and are now in Force. Your Excellency says, that when the Colony applied to King William for a second Charter, they knew the Oath the King had taken, which was to govern them according to the Statutes in Parliament, and (which your Excellency here omits) *the Laws and Customs of the same.* By the Laws and Customs of Parliament, the People of England freely debate and consent to such Statutes as are made by themselves or their chosen Representatives. This is a Law or Custom which all Mankind may justly challenge as their *inherent* Right.[35] According to this Law the King has an undoubted Right to govern us. Your Excellency upon Recollection surely will not infer from hence, that it was the Sense of our Predecessors that there was to remain a Supremacy in the English Parliament, or a full Power and Authority to make Laws binding upon us in all Cases whatever, in that Parliament where we cannot *debate* and *deliberate* upon the Necessity or Expediency of any Law, and consequently without our Consent, and as it may probably happen destructive of the first Law of Society, the Good of the Whole. You tell us that "after the Assumption of all the Powers of Government, by Virtue of the new Charter, an Act passed for the reviving for a limited Time all the local Laws of the Massachusetts-Bay and

[35] The meaning of this sentence is not clear. If a reference to natural law, it is inexplicitly inserted in a discussion of constitutional law. Perhaps it is evidence that John Adams wrote this rejoinder and Samuel Adams edited the final version. The entire paragraph reflects John Adams's legal theory. The sentence above relates to propaganda or political declamations of the type associated with Samuel Adams.

New-Plymouth respectively, not repugnant to the Laws of England. And at the same Session an act passed establishing Naval Officers, that all undue Trading contrary to an Act of Parliament—may be prevented." Among the Acts that were then revived we may reasonably suppose was that whereby Provision was made to give Force to this Act of Parliament in the Province. The Establishment therefore of the Naval Officers was to aid the Execution of an Act of Parliament for the Observance of which within the Colony the Assembly had before made Provision after free Debates with their own Consent and by their own Act.

The Act of Parliament passed in 1741,[36] for putting an End to several unwarrantable Schemes, mentioned by your Excellency, was designed for the general Good, and if the Validity of it was not disputed, it cannot be urged as a Concession of the supreme Authority, to make Laws binding on us *in all Cases whatever:* But if the Design of it was for the general Benefit of the Province, it was in one Respect at least greatly complained of by the Persons more immediately affected by it; and to remedy the Inconvenience, the Legislative of this Province pass'd an Act, directly militating with it.[37] Which is the strongest evidence, that altho' they may have submitted *sub silentio* to some Acts of Parliament that they conceived might operate for their Benefit, they did not conceive themselves bound by any of its Acts which they judged would operate to the Injury even of Individuals.

Your Excellency has not thought proper to attempt to confute the Reasoning of a learned Writer on the Laws of Nature and Nations, quoted by us on this Occasion,[38] to shew that the Authority of the Legislature does not extend so far as the Fundamentals of the Constitution. We are unhappy in not having your Remarks upon the Reasoning of that great Man; and until it is confuted, we shall remain of the Opinion, that the Fundamentals of the Constitution being excepted from the Commission of the Legislators, none of the Acts or Doings of the General Assembly, however deliberate and solemn, could avail to change them, if the People have not in very express Terms given them the Power to do it; and that much less ought their Acts and Doings however numerous, which barely refer to Acts of Parliament made ex-

[36] 14 George II, cap. 37.
[37] "An Act for the more speedy Finishing of the Land-Bank or Manufacturing Scheme." Chapter 17, Laws of 1743/44, 3 *Acts and Resolves*, at 118–21.
[38] Vattel.

pressly to relate to us, to be taken as an Acknowledgment that we are subject to the Supreme Authority of Parliament.

We shall sum up our own sentiments in the Words of that learned Writer Mr. Hooker, in his Ecclesiastical Policy, as quoted by Mr. Locke,[39] "The lawful Power of making Laws to command whole political Societies of Men, belonging so properly to the same intire Societies, that for any Prince or Potentate of what Kind soever, to exercise the same of himself, and not from express Commission immediately and personally received from God, is no better *than mere Tyranny.* Laws therefore they are not which *publick Approbation* hath not made so,[40] for "Laws human of what Kind soever are available by Consent."[41] "Since men naturally have no full and perfect Power to command whole politick Multitudes of Men, therefore, utterly without our Consent we could in such Sort be at no Man's Commandment living. And to be commanded we do not consent, when that Society whereof we be a Part, hath at any Time before consented."[42] We think your Excellency has not proved, either that the Colony is a Part of the politick Society of England, or that it has ever consented that the Parliament of England or Great Britain should make Laws binding upon us in all Cases whatever, whether made expressly to refer to us or not.

We cannot help before we conclude, expressing our great Concern, that your Excellency has thus repeatedly, in a Manner insisted upon our free sentiments on Matters of so delicate a Nature, and weighty Importance. The Question appears to us to be no other, than Whether we are the Subjects of absolute unlimited Power, or of a free Government formed on the Principles of the English Constitution. If your Excellency's Doctrine be true, the People of this Province hold their Lands of the Crown and People

---

[39] It is indicative of how the actual context of the debate differed from the taught preconceptions with which many historians have viewed the prerevolutionary controversy, that here, the only time John Locke is cited by the whig side, he serves not as authority but as a means by which Richard Hooker could be quoted conveniently. Locke's influence upon the formulations of American whig theory has been grossly exaggerated. All of the words quoted here come from Hooker. For Adams's source see Locke, *Two Treatises,* at 282–83 [Book II, Chap. 11, Sec. 134].

[40] Hooker, *Ecclesiastical Politie,* at 28.

[41] Ibid., at 29.

[42] Ibid.

of England, and their Lives, Liberties and Properties are at their Disposal; and that even by Compact and their own Consent. They are subject to the King as the Head *alterius Populi* of another People, in whose Legislative they have no Voice or Interest. They are indeed said to have a Constitution and a Legislative of their own, but your Excellency has explained it into a mere Phantom; limitted, controuled, superceded and nullified at the Will of another. Is this the Constitution which so charmed our Ancestors, that as your Excellency has informed us, they kept a Day of solemn Thanksgiving to Almighty God when they received it? And were they men of so little Discernment, such Children in Understanding, as to please themselves with the Imagination that they were blessed with the same Rights and Liberties which natural born Subjects in England enjoyed, when at the same Time they had fully consented to be ruled and ordered by a Legislative a Thousand Leagues distant from them, which cannot be supposed to be sufficiently acquainted with their Circumstances, if concerned for their Interest, and which they, cannot be in any Sense represented.

THE SURREJOINDER
OF THE GOVERNOR

INTRODUCTION

"The debate," Thomas Hutchinson's recent biographer has written, "went on in exchanges of messages for two months, until it exhausted the knowledge, ingenuity, and patience of all involved."[1] Certainly Governor Hutchinson was exhausted. By the terms he, himself, had set, the burden of proof had been on him. It had been his task to persuade the whigs, not theirs to persuade him. As he read the two rejoinders, he saw that for a second time he had failed. Yet he was game to make one last try.

That Governor Hutchinson was willing to write a surrejoinder and risk making the assembly's rejection of his arguments even more decisive than it already was, tells us one of two things. First, Hutchinson may have been conceding a fact he would not acknowledge even to himself: that his whig opponents were men of open minds and political good will, that they could be persuaded by convincing constitutional arguments. If not, then Hutchinson must have been acting on a belief the opposite of one he stated in the sur-

---

[1] 1 *Pamphlets of the American Revolution 1750–1776*, at 133 (Bernard Bailyn ed., 1965).

145

rejoinder. "I am sensible," he said, "that nice Distinctions of civil Rights and legal Constitutions are far above the Reach of the Bulk of Mankind to comprehend." Hutchinson could not have meant what he said if he did not think the whigs in the council and the house receptive to persuasion. The only other practical purpose for writing the surrejoinder was to reach their constituents, the people of the small rural towns of inland Massachusetts and the Maine district. And if he was speaking to them, Hutchinson surely thought that "nice Distinctions of civil Rights and legal Constitutions" were not beyond their reach, and that they acted on and were motivated by constitutional principles.

THE DOCUMENT

On Saturday the 6th of March, *his Excellency was pleas'd to put an End to the Session, after delivering the following* SPEECH *to both Houses, viz.*

Gentlemen of the Council, and

Gentlemen of the House of Representatives,

I think it incumbent on me to make some Observations, before I put an End to the Session, upon your last Messages to me on the Subject of your Constitutional Dependance upon the Supreme Authority of the British Dominions. As the Council admit a partial Dependence, and suppose it to be consistent with the Principles and Nature of Government, I shall only endeavour very briefly to shew the contrary.

In your first Message, Gentlemen of the Council, you made some Strictures upon the Nature of the Supreme Authority in Government, both divine and human, the latter of which you determined could not be absolute and unlimitted. I thought the Distinction between divine and human Power not pertinent, and in Answer to you, I only remarked, that I had given you no Reason to suppose I intended a more absolute Power in Parliament than what is founded in the Nature of Government, and this, in your second Message, you construe an Acquiescence in your Reasons, which it certainly was not. You go on however to explain your Meaning by asserting, that "what is usually denominated the Supreme Authority of a Nation must be limited in its Acts to the Objects that are properly or constitutionally Cognizable by it."

Before you thus defined the Nature of Supreme Authority, I wish you had considered more fully what Objects there can be in a Government which are not cognizable by such Authority. You instance in a *subordinate* Power in Government which, whilst it keeps within its Limits, is not subject to the Controul of the *supreme* Power. Is there no Inconsistency in supposing a *subordinate* Power without a Power *superior* to it? Must it not so far as it is without Controul be, itself, Supreme?[1]

It is essential to the Being of Government that a Power should always exist which no other Power within such Government can have Right to withstand or controul: Therefore, when the word *Power* relates to the Supreme Authority of Government it must be understood *absolute* and *unlimited*.

If we cannot agree in these Principles which no sensible Writer upon Government has before denied, and if you are still of Opinion that two Jurisdictions, each of them having a Share in the Supreme Power, are compatible in the same State, it can be to no Purpose to Reason or Argue upon the other Parts of your Message. Its enough to observe that this Disagreement in our Principles will have its Influence upon all the Deductions which are made from them.

I will also consider the last Message from you, Gentlemen of the House of Representatives, upon the same Subject, in as few words as the Importance of it will admit.

[1] Reasoning from ideal models rather than experience, Hutchinson believed that the logic of his theoretical premises made untenable the council's argument. The problem was not only that there was no imperial supreme court to which disputes could be appealed, but that (by Hutchinson's conception) a judicial tribunal empowered to arbitrate constitutional disputes and limit the action of government was an impossibility—unless that judicial tribunal was also the supreme sovereign authority. The house, he thought, recognizing the impossibility and impelled by the same logic, had asserted independence from parliament. "The house saw the difficulty they should be involved in by admitting two supreme powers, for if there be no umpire to judge when one or the other exceeded its just limits, contests must soon arise, and one or other would soon become the sole power; or otherwise both would be dissolved, and anarchy take place of government. And if an umpire be admitted, the umpire would be supreme, and the other two subordinate. In order to maintain their own authority, they found it necessary to exclude all others." 3 Hutchinson, *Massachusetts Bay,* at 274.

You say you have not discovered that the Principles advanced by the Town of Boston are unwarrantable by the Constitution. Whether they are or are not, will depend upon the Determination of the Point which you are now controverting. Your not having discover'd that the other Towns and Districts in the Province, were invited by the Town of Boston to adopt their Principles, must proceed from Inattention. Have not the Doings of that Town been sent through the Province, accompanied with a circular Letter, "desiring a free Communication of Sentiments," and, among other Expressions of the like Tendency, lamenting the Extinction of Ardor for civil and religious Liberty if it should be the general Voice of the Province, that the Rights as stated do not belong to them, and trusting that this cannot be the Case. If this is not inviting to adopt their Principles, I have mistaken their Sense and Meaning. The consequent Doings of so many other Towns shew that they understood them as I have done. I am sure I have no Disposition to represent unfavourably the Doings of any Town in the Province.

You assert "that it is the indisputable Right of all or any of His Majesty's Subjects in this Province *regularly and orderly* to meet together to state the Grievances they labour under." &c. I never denied it. Does it follow that it is *regular* and *orderly* for the Inhabitants of Towns, in their Corporate Capacity, to meet and determine upon Points which the Law gives them no Power to act upon? You have not asserted that it is, but you have not declared that it is not, as I thought a Regard to the Peace and Order of the Province made our Duty.

If the Fundamentals of our Government were not disputed, these Irregularities would appear to you in a very strong Light and you would join in discountenancing them.

To support your Principle that you hold your Lands and derive your Authority of Government from the *Kings* of England and not from the *Crown* of England you have very largely handled the Doctrine of Feudal Tenures. I observed to you in my last Speech that you had been misled by the Authority of an anonimous Pamphlet. I am now obliged to observe that you are again misled by having a general View of this Doctrine brought before you, as it respects States or Governments under absolute Monarchs, and not as it is connected with or grafted upon the English Constitution. I shall not therefore spend Time in examining the Principles of your System, it being immaterial to the Point between us whether they are just or not. Instead thereof I will, in as brief and clear Terms as I can, lay this Doctrine before you as it relates to the Government of England.

Let me then observe to you, that from the Nature of Government a Supreme Legislative Power must always exist over all the Parts and all the Affairs of every Dominion—that in absolute Monarchies the Legislative and executive Powers are united in the Prince or Monarch—that in the English Constitution there is, and always has been, a Legislative Power distinct from the regal or executive Power—that the Feudal System, in your View of it and without correcting, could not be introduced into the English Government without changing the Constitution from a mixed to an absolute monarchical Government—that this System nevertheless has been introduced, the Constitution of a mixed Government still remaining, and consequently the System has been corrected or altered. What this Alteration has been will appear from Historical Facts. Before the Reign of William the First the Traces of Feudal Tenure are faint, the evidence of a Legislative Power, an Assembly or Council of Wise Men, distinct from the Regal Power is strong and sufficient. After William had obtained the Crown, the other Nations of Europe being under this System, & particularly his Dominions in Normandy, and Wars being more frequent & Commerce small, and the Means of furnishing Money, the Sinews of War, difficult if not impracticable, meerly for the Defence of the Kingdom this Polity was so far established as that all the Landholders were made to contribute, by Military or other Services, to the Defence of the State, and for this Purpose, and by a Fiction only, the Lands were in Form acknowledged to have been originally in the King and held of him by his Subjects, and by this Form subjected to a supposed just Proportion of the Defence and Support of the Kingdom. This Establishment appears to have been made, not by an Act of Regal Power alone but by the Authority of the great Council of the Nation or Assembly of the Realm, and the Legislative Authority still remained, according to its Nature, paramount and above all Powers in the Dominion, and accordingly from Time to Time the Abuses of the Feudal Power either in the Sovereign or in such as held under him were corrected by the Supreme Legislative, and Magna Charta itself was framed and agreed upon, principally if not altogether for this Purpose. In succeeding Ages, as Commerce and Money increased and the Means of supporting War became more easy, these Military Services were gradually taken away, either, by Purchase or commuting for other Services or certain Rents, so that at the Period when America was first granted, the Remains were inconsiderable and the Lands of the Kingdom were held, generally, by what is called Socage Tenure, or in other Words, an Acknowledgment of Fidelity to the Sovereign, and a certain Rent which was in Name only, or of Value so inconsiderable as not to be demanded. The original Claim in the Sovereign, whether at first a Fiction or not, so far remained as that all Forfeitures, all Escheats, all new discovered Lands accrued to him, unless the Supreme Legislative should limit the Right to them, or otherwise dispose of them. This was the State of Feudal Tenure in England at the Time when the first Charter was granted, and the Difference between your System and mine will appear by this familiar Instance: Louis the 13 of France, I think the same Year the Massachusetts Patentees obtained the Grant of that Colony, by a Royal Edict granted to one Hundred Associates the Country of Canada, with Powers of Government and all the Privileges of natural born Subjects of France to all who should go and Inhabit or be Born there, with other very great Powers and Privileges. This, then, appears to be the different State of the People of the two Colonies. Louis, being an absolute Monarch, the Regal and Legislative Power were united in him. The Inhabitants of Canada therefore were subject to him and to every succeeding King of France as their Supreme Lord who, by Virtue of his uncontroulable Power, might at any Time revoke the Royal Edict at Pleasure, or dissolve any Charter whatsoever even though like the famous Edict of Nantes it had been declared irrevocable. Charles, having in him the regal Power only, could Grant no more than was in him, and the Legislative Power which was in the Parliament must still remain there, and consequently the Subjects of England continued when in the Colony still subject to the regal constitutional Power of Charles and the supreme Legislative Power of Parliament. And, I think, nothing is more certain than that the constitutional Restraint of the regal Power in Charles prevented the Charter from being revoked and annulled in less than Ten Years after the Date of it.

If this brief Account of Feudal Tenure, as it is Part of the English Constitution, be just, as I shall think it is until I have better Authority than any I have yet seen to the contrary, the Fabrick which you have raised will still fail of Support, for it wholly depends upon very different Principles, and upon what you hope I do not mean to introduce, viz. the Feudal System in its Perfection. If this Support fails, there is but little Occasion for me to remark upon the other Parts of your Message, and I shall pass them over, except such as may tend to make wrong Impressions upon any unwary Readers.

You cannot conceive "why the King has not the same Right to alienate and dispose of Countries acquired by the Discovery of his Subjects as he has to restore upon a Treaty of Peace Countries acquired in War carried on at the charge of the Nation, or to sell and deliver up any Part of his Dominions against the general Sense of the Nation." I will venture to conjecture a Reason. By the English Constitution the sole Power of making War and Peace is in the King. It often happens that the restoring and ceding Acquisitions made in War is absolutely necessary to the Reestablishment of Peace, and if the King was restrained from such Restorations or Cessions an unsucessful War might be perpetuated to the Destruction of the Kingdom. This Power therefore seems necessarily to result from this Prerogative of the Crown. And for selling any Part of the Dominions against the general Sense of the Nation I never supposed it to be a Part of the Prerogative, but have called it an Act of *Power,* by which I thought no candid Reader would understand any Thing but *meer Power.*[2]

[2] Hutchinson was referring to the most basic distinction in eighteenth-century constitutional theory: "that *Power* abstracted from *Right* cannot give a just title to Dominion." Bland, *An Inquiry,* at 25. Referring to the prerevolutionary controversy a writer pointed out that although "the Parliament has Power to deprive me of any Part of my Property they think fit, and to subject me to every possible Degree of Misery and Wretchedness; but if I have done nothing to deserve it, *Power only* gives them no *Right* to do it." [Fothergill,] *Considerations,* at 19–20. The distinction, therefore, was between "power" and "right," and right was equated with "law." An "unconstitutional" act of parliament was an act of "meer power." Resolves of Sheffield, 12 January 1773, *Evening-Post,* 15 February 1773, at 2, col. 1. Similarly see, *Boston Gazette,* 4 May 1767, at 3, col. 1. What was unconstitutional might, by power, be made lawful either because it could not be resisted or had to be obeyed. "By Law all Lands are originally in the Crown and flow from it to their Subjects, on what Terms the Crown thinks fit, but after these Lands are granted, it is not in the Power of the Crown to resume these Grants; and if the Crown and Parliament jointly should deprive any Subject of their [*sic*] Property or Privileges, it would be unjust, tho' that Subject had not Power to resist." *Gazette & News-Letter,* 6 February 1766, at 1, col. 3. Or as Hutchinson himself wrote of parliament's claim to tax Americans: "When this first became a topick for conversation, few or none were willing to admit the right, but the power and, from thence the obligation to submit none would deny." Letter from Chief Justice Thomas Hutchinson to Former Governor Thomas Pownall, 8 March 1766, Morgan, *Prologue,* at 123.

Your attempt to shew that new discovered Countries do not become Part of the State, from the Authority of Puffendorff [*sic*], &c. will fail, because the Instance given by him of a Colony erected into a separate Common Wealth plainly appears by the Context to be by the Leave or Consent of the Parent State, and it does not appear that the other Cases were not so.

Your Remark upon the Authority I bring to shew that the Colony, being feudatory, is under the Government of the King's Laws, is very singular. You suppose it must mean the King's Laws *absolutely,* or as you explain it, not the Laws of Parliament. Do any of you remember ever to have seen the Expression, *the King's Laws,* meaning the King of England, used in any other Sense than *the Laws of the Realm*? You say I have not named the Authority. The Case I refer to is the King against Crowle, in the 2d. Vol Burrow's Reports, and for the Authority, which you will find mentioned there, I am not able to name a greater.[3]

I would pass over in Silence your Attempt to shew that Allegiance is due to the natural Person and not to the Body Politick of the King, if I had not been well informed that the artificial Reasoning of Lord Chief Justice Coke upon the Doctrine of Allegiance, in the noted Case of Calvin, as you have recited it, had great Weight with some of the Members of the House. But have you recited this Case truly? After all the Refinements on this Subject does it appear that they can amount to any Thing more than that Allegiance is not due to the Politick Capacity *only*? And is it not expressly said that the natural Person of the King is ever accompanied with the Politick Capacity, and the Politick Capacity as it were appropriated to the Natural Capacity? Or have you any clear Idea of Allegiance to a King in his natural Capacity without any Relation to his political Capacity? From this Authority misunderstood you infer that I am mistaken in supposing your Allegiance to be due to the *Crown* of England. Without any Refinements, it is plain that it was one Condition, on the Performance whereof the first Charter depended, that Allegiance should be borne to King Charles his Heirs and *Successors*. Wherever therefore the Succession to the Crown shall go there Allegiance is to follow. The Condition in the second Charter is the same, and this is enough for my Purpose, which was to shew that in whatever Person the Regal Authority shall be, there your Allegiance is due.

[3] Lord Mansfield.

I wish you had omitted all you have said upon this Subject, for neither the Reasoning of Lord Coke, nor the Declarations of the Judges, in any Measure tend to the Purpose for which you produce them.

Your Assertion that Parliament, in regulating the Fishery, had nothing in View but to prevent a Monopoly of the Sea, and claimed no Authority over the Plantations or Lands in America, has only your own Authority to support it. It appears from the Debates in Parliament, that it was the Refusal of the Patentees to suffer Fish to be dried upon the Land within their Patent, by any Person who had not Licence from them, which was complained of as a Grievance, and the Bill was brought in to remove this Grievance: The King might very well refuse his Assent, not because Parliament had no Jurisdiction, but because he did not think fit to join with the Lords and Commons in an Act which invalidated or abridged those Privileges in a Patent of Lands which by his Royal Prerogative he had a Right to grant.

I will make no particular Remarks upon those Parts of your Message which relate to the Sense the People have had of their Constitution, as there can be no End to Disputes upon Facts which by small Deviations from the true State of them may be made to serve one Side or the other.

It is evident that the first Settlers of this Colony left England with a just Sense of their Dependance—that the Sense continued until the Principles of Anarchy in England spread in America, and it is conceded that these Principles were avowed by many of the Inhabitants here for near twenty Years after they were exploded in England. It is equally certain, that at the Time of the Revolution the People returned to a just Sense of the Supremacy of Parliament, and I think I may very safely say that the oldest Person in the Province has never heard the Supremacy called in Question until within a few Years past.

You again express your Concern that I should thus repeatedly insist upon your giving your free Sentiments on so delicate a Subject as the Authority of Parliament. In the Beginning of your Message you vindicate the Town of Boston & the other Towns in the Province, which have met together and determined upon the same Subject, and made their Proceedings Matter of Record and published them in News-Papers; and yet in the Close of it you assert that the Subject is too delicate and of too great Importance for you to consider. Certainly then it must have been extremely irregular in the Towns to take upon them separately to determine Points which they had no Authority to determine, and in this Way to influence if not determine the Acts and Doings of their Representatives in General Assembly, who cannot have the same Freedom of thinking and acting, after their Constituents have determined and resolved, as they had before.

Gentlemen of the Council
and House of Representatives,

I am sensible that nice Distinctions of civil Rights and legal Constitutions are far above the Reach of the Bulk of mankind to comprehend. There are, however, a few plain fundamental Principles of Government which carry within themselves such Evidence as cannot be resisted, and are no sooner proposed than assented to—Such as these—That in every Government there must be somewhere a supreme uncontroulable Power, an absolute Authority to decide and determine—That two such Powers cannot coexist, but necessarily will make two distinct States—That in a State of Society we give up Part of our natural Liberty in order to secure that legal Freedom which it is the great End of Government to maintain and preserve—That a Right in Individuals or Parts of a Government to judge of the Decisions of the Supreme Authority and to submit or not submit as they think proper cannot consist with a State of Government and must work the Dissolution of it. Whilst these Principles had their due Influence we enjoyed all that Freedom and all those other Blessings which a State of Government will admit of. Our Connection with our Parent State secured these Blessings to us, and by Means of a nominal Dependence we possessed as great a Share of real Freedom as the Parent State itself upon which we are said to depend.

I have laid before you, Gentlemen, what appeared to me to be the true Constitution of the Province, and recommended an Adherence to it because I believed it would restore us to and continue us in that happy State in which we flourished so long a Course of Years.

Certainly it is of the utmost Importance to you that these Points should be settled, for I know of no Maxim in the Law of greater Truth than this. *Where the Constitution is contested and the Laws are vague and uncertain, there, will be the greatest Slavery.*

CONCLUSION

The debates delighted Arthur Lee of Virginia. "The champion of despotism, Mr. H. has in the opinion of all mankind cried *Craven,*" Lee assured Samuel Adams.[1] John Adams agreed. "Mr. Hutchinson really made a meager figure in that dispute," he concluded. "He had waded beyond his depth. He had wholly misunderstood the legal doctrine of allegiance."[2] "I stand amazed at the Governor, for forcing on this Controversy. He will not be thanked for this. His Ruin and Destruction must spring out of it, either from the Ministry and Parliament on one Hand, or from his Countrymen, on the other. He has reduced himself to a most ridiculous State of Distress . . . and seems in the utmost Agony."[3] Hutchinson's mistake, some whigs believed, was to have opened the debates. "The Ministry," Thomas Cushing understood, "are greatly chagrined at his officiousness, their intention having been to let all controversy subside,

---

[1] Letter from Arthur Lee to Samuel Adams, 13 October 1773, 1 Lee, *Arthur Lee,* at 237.

[2] Letter from John Adams to William Tutor, 8 March 1817, 2 Adams, *Works,* at 313.

[3] Entry for 4 March 1773, 2 *Diary and Autobiography,* at 77.

and by degrees suffer matters to return to their old channel."[4]

Governor Hutchinson may have suspected that his reputation in London had been tarnished, for he wrote Lord Dartmouth claiming that he had halted the tide of town meetings. After people read his first address, he boasted, not "more than one or two" towns had met to adopt the Boston Declaration.[5] A suggestion of what he may have really been thinking was revealed in a long letter—as much an apologia as a report—sent to General Thomas Gage. "I am afraid," he explained, "that the controversy I have been engaged in which has appeared in all the news papers will leave some impressions to my disadvantage where the motives to it are not known." As he had with Dartmouth, Hutchinson insisted to Gage that he had arrested the spread of the Boston Declaration,[6] and more significantly, by forcing the whigs to state their constitutional imperatives, had exposed them to the view of a previously misinformed public. "By their trifling distinctions and shameful evasions," he wrote of the briefs of the house of representatives, "they have dishonoured themselves extremely, and by their open avowal of principles incompatible with any degree of subordination I think they must open the eyes of the nation and lose every Advocate they had there." Despite these confident claims a note of despair crept into the letter. He was justifying his actions to General Gage, Hutchinson explained, "as I wish to retain a share of your esteem."[7]

The governor later claimed that before he commenced

[4]Cushing, "Letter," at 360. "[H]e has thereby defeated the favorite Design of the Ministry, which was to lull the people into Security, and for the effecting of which Design he had before thought himself, or endeavor[e]d to make Administration believe he was entitled to so great a Share of Merit." Letter from Samuel Adams to Arthur Lee, 9 April 1773, 3 Adams, *Writings,* at 20.

[5]Letter from Governor Thomas Hutchinson to the earl of Dartmouth, 22 February 1773, 6 *Revolution Documents,* at 89.

[6]"I have . . . stopped the Town in their progress and prevented the proposed application to the other Governments." Letter from Governor Thomas Hutchinson to General Thomas Gage, 7 March 1773, Gage, *Papers.*

[7]Ibid.

the debates the "design was approved of."[8] He meant by Lord Dartmouth who, as late as the time Hutchinson was working on the replication, was complaining of the Boston Declaration, warning that it was "of a very serious nature" with "a direct tendency to encourage violence and tumult."[9] Two months later, when he had read the answers of the council and house, Dartmouth confessed that the situation was much worse than he had thought. Constitutional principles he had attributed to a small number of Bostonians, he realized, were held by elected leaders from all over the colony. "After so public an avowal in the representative body of the people of doctrines subversive of every principle of the constitutional dependence of the colonies upon the kingdom, it is vain to hope that they will be induced by argument and persuasion to yield due obedience to the laws of Parliament and to acquiesce in those arrangements which the King, consulting the welfare and happiness of his subjects, has thought fit to adopt."[10]

Dartmouth concluded that Hutchinson had made a political mistake opening up the constitution for debate. He had hoped the governor would "remove those prejudices which the artificers of faction had endeavoured to fix on the minds of the country members." He agreed that Hutchinson had to "call upon the Council and House of Representatives to be explicit with regard to their sentiments" concerning the Boston Declaration, especially after its endorsement by other towns such as Salem, Plymouth, and Roxbury. "But how far it was or was not expedient to enter so fully in your speech into an exposition of your own opinion in respect to the principles of the constitution of the colony I am not able to judge; but whatever the effect of that speech may be, it was certainly justified in the inten-

---

[8] 3 Hutchinson, *Massachusetts Bay,* at 276.
[9] Letter from the earl of Dartmouth to Governor Thomas Hutchinson, 3 February 1773, quoted in Cary, *Warren,* at 115–16.
[10] Letter from Dartmouth to Hutchinson, 10 April 1773, 4 *Revolution Documents,* at 295, quoted in B. D. Bargar, *Lord Dartmouth and the American Revolution* 87 (1965).

tion."[11] Coming from Lord Dartmouth these were strong words and Hutchinson felt the rebuke. "It gives me pain," he wrote the colonial secretary, "that any step which I have taken with the most sincere intention to promote his Majesty's service, should be judged to have a contrary effect."[12]

Thomas Hutchinson persisted in the belief that the cause of imperial government had not been "disserved" by his speeches.[13] Years later, as an exile in London, he asked the opinion of "a person of the first rank, as well as reputation, in the law in England," who may have been Edward Thurlow, attorney general and later lord chancellor. Hutchinson was gratified on being told that his constitutional argument was "a very succinct and judicious digest of the argument upon the relation of the colonies to the metropolis."[14] We may wonder, however, if Hutchinson had many more British admirers. Benjamin Franklin did not think so,[15] a belief he acted on by having the answers of the council and house published in London.[16] When Dartmouth suggested legislation to lay the Massachusetts assembly "under some Inconveniences" until the two houses rescinded their claims of independence from parliament, Franklin assured him it would prove a futile effort. Constitutional discussion could not revert to what it had been before Hutchinson delivered his address. "If they were even to wish the Dispute obliter-

[11] Letter from Dartmouth to Hutchinson, 3 March 1773, 6 *Revolution Documents,* at 95.

[12] Letter from Hutchinson to Dartmouth, 12 June 1773, quoted in Hosmer, *Hutchinson,* at 251.

[13] Letter from Hutchinson to Dartmouth, 1 June 1773, 6 *Revolution Documents,* at 321.

[14] 3 Hutchinson, *Massachusetts Bay,* at 275.

[15] "The Governor was certainly out in his Politics, if he hoped to recommend himself there, by entering upon that Dispute with the Assembly. His Imprudence in bringing it at all upon the *tapis,* and his bad Management of it, are almost equally censured. The Council and Assembly on the other hand have, by their Coolness, Clearness, and Force of their Answers, gained great Reputation." Letter from Benjamin Franklin to Reverend Samuel Cooper, 7 July 1773, 6 Franklin, *Writings,* at 89.

[16] Letter from Benjamin Franklin to Speaker Thomas Cushing, 6 May 1773, 6 Franklin, *Writings,* at 48.

ated, they cannot withdraw their Answers till he first withdraws his Speech, which methinks would be an awkward Operation, that perhaps he will hardly be directed to perform." [17]

On the whole, most American whigs, given a choice, would have preferred Hutchinson not to have started the debates. Those who were lawyers knew what the ultimate constitutional question was, but as good lawyers they had hoped to avoid stating it. Whether they could do so was up to the parliament of Great Britain. If parliament did not assert the power, Americans would not deny the right. [18] Whenever possible, protests against parliamentary innovations were stated in words politically positive yet legally neutral by denying the right without specifically raising the question of sovereignty, the one contention parliament could not accept. An example of this tactic occurred during the debates. The day after the house voted its rejoinder, it passed a resolution denouncing the latest constitutional innovation by London: crown salaries for colonial judges. The argument was stated not in absolutest language rejecting parliamentary supremacy, but in language permitting parliament to retreat. To have stated flatly that parliament lacked the sovereign authority to grant colonial salaries would have placed parliamentary lawyers in a position where they would have had to advise their colleagues that there could be no compromise. Better therefore to state the issue without claiming independence from parliament's jurisdiction. It was an argument made easier by the fact that although parliament had authorized the salaries in 1767, the ministry had only recently made the decision to grant them. It was a political fact opening the way to constitutional restraint, and the Massachusetts house protested

---

[17] Ibid., at 49.

[18] Thus Thomas Cushing told Arthur Lee: "This dispute, though it may in some measure retard the redress of our grievance, has upon the whole been of advantage to America. We have gained ground by it. However, I entirely agree with you in sentiment, (as expressed in your letter to Mr. Adams,) that it is not worth our while to press the matter too far, at this time." Cushing, "Letter," at 360.

crown stipends for the judiciary on the ground that they
would deprive Americans of certain English constitutional
rights, not on the ultimate question of parliamentary sovereignty.

> RESOLVED, That the admitting any Authority to make Laws
> binding on the People of this Province in all Cases whatso-
> ever, saving the General Court or Assembly, is inconsistent
> with the Spirit of our free Constitution, and is Repugnant to
> one of the most essential Clauses in our Charter, whereby the
> Inhabitants are intitled to all the Liberties of free and natural
> born Subject[s], to all Intents, Constructions and Purposes
> whatsoever, as if they had been born within Realm of En-
> gland.—It reduces the People to the absolute Will and Dis-
> posal of a Legislature in which they can have no Voice, and
> who may make it their Interest to oppress & enslave them.[19]

It is important to realize that the house of representatives
with this resolution was not retreating from or being inconsistent with the arguments made in its answer and rejoinder. It was not necessary in the resolution to deny parliamentary sovereignty to the extent Hutchinson forced the
house to deny it in the debates and there was reason not to
do so. The distinction is vital because it was vital in 1773,
but, unfortunately, the training of our historians has led
them to overlook its significance. We, however, will never
understand what was being said and what writers intended
to say during the prerevolutionary controversy until we pay
heed to the words that participants used and ask what they
meant by those words and what ideas they sought to convey.

We should also heed words employed by today's writers
about the Revolution as they may mislead us even more. A
recent commentator asserted that the debates of 1773 were
concerned with "political beliefs," that Hutchinson's mistake
was failing to realize that everyone did not agree with "his
own fundamental political beliefs."[20] The problem arises

[19] Session of 3 March 1773, *Journal of the House*, at 281.
[20] Robert D. Brown, *Revolutionary Politics in Massachusetts: The Boston Committee of Correspondence and the Towns, 1772–1774*, at 89 (1970).

from the decision to use the word "political" rather than "constitutional," a decision that may have been intentional but most likely was careless. If the principles that Thomas Hutchinson stated in his three speeches can be termed "political beliefs," there is no distinction between "constitutional" and "political." To label his beliefs "political" not only clouds our perception of what was argued and what was at issue, it causes us to think of Hutchinson's ideas in an entirely different context from the one in which he expected them to be understood. Interpreters of the American Revolution have for too long been certain that it could not have been precipitated by constitutional motivations. Their search for other causes explains why the briefs of 1773 have not been accorded by history books the significance they had to contemporaries. No matter how we may misrepresent the prerevolutionary controversy as an economic, political, or nationalistic movement, those who argued it knew they were involved in a constitutional dispute. Thomas Hutchinson had started the debates hoping to divert Massachusetts whigs "from their main object, tearing the constitution to pieces."[21] He was thinking primarily of the Boston town meeting. After reading Hutchinson's three speeches, the voters of that same town concluded it was the governor not they who was tearing the constitution to pieces. It was, a second Boston meeting resolved (referring to Hutchinson's central constitution premise), "impossible to be shown that the Parliament of Great Britain can exercise 'the Powers of Legislation for the Colonists in all Cases whatever' consistently with the Rights which belong to the Colonists as Men as Christians & as Subjects, or without destroying the foundation of their own Constitution."[22]

If we must judge the briefs, it could be difficult not to conclude that the constitutional cause championed by Thomas Hutchinson would have been better served had

[21] Letter from Governor Thomas Hutchinson to Commodore James Gambier, 14 February 1773, Hosmer, *Hutchinson*, at 250.
[22] Report of the Town of Boston, 23 March 1773, in 3 Adams, *Writings*, at 10.

they remained unwritten. It is not that the governor of Massachusetts Bay misunderstood the British constitution. He understood it better than did Samuel Adams and perhaps as well as did John Adams. His failing did not even arise from the heart; it cannot be said that his error was that of a nonwhig arguing whig principles. Thomas Hutchinson was a whig in the limited sense that he gloried in the whig constitution. He was not a whig in the American sense, for his view of the constitution was rigid, and he did not appreciate the continuing vitality of English constitutional dynamism. "The constitution of England, as it now stands, was fixed at the Revolution, in 1688," Charles Inglis would one day write in answer to the arguments of Tom Paine. "What is it to us, what the constitution of England was two or three hundred or a thousand years ago? That constitution, as fixed at the revolution, as it *now* stands, is what we are interested in."[23]

Inglis's words could easily have been written by Thomas Hutchinson. He, too, boasted of a revolutionary constitution that was static. If the concepts seem a strange mix, it is because we are viewing them from a whiggish not a Hutchinsonian perspective. He gloried in the same constitutional history that motivated his whig opponents and took pride in claiming as his inheritance the same rights of Englishmen that they claimed. Constitutional history was cherished because it revealed the forces and the reason for creating those rights, and the constitution Thomas Hutchinson defended had been a product of both that history and the struggle by the English to guarantee those rights. What he did not see was that the Glorious Revolution had erected constitutional barriers protecting English but not American rights. Due to the constitutional reality that the threat to freedom in seventeenth-century England had been the crown, the guarantor of those rights in Great Britain had become the sovereign parliament. That was the irony once

[23] [Charles Inglis,] *The True Interest of America Impartially Stated, in Certain Strictures on a Pamphlet Intitled Common Sense* 15 (2d. ed. 1776).

parliament decided it was supreme in the colonies as well as in England and Scotland. The guarantor of rights at home became the threat to freedom in North America. Parliament became for colonial whigs what the crown had been for Puritans, common lawyers, and parliamentarians in early Stuart England, and the colonial whigs were invoking the constitutional tradition of seventeenth-century Puritans, common lawyers, and parliamentarians. Thomas Hutchinson understood that constitutional history but missed its application to his own times.[24]

We have been considering a constitutional debate, and should be tempted to leave it on a note of abstract principle. Yet it is not unrealistic to depart from the legal and end by considering the personal. The American Revolution was a personal tragedy for many individuals and among the most tragic was Thomas Hutchinson. Perhaps all that is being said is that he was a child of the Glorious Revolution who could not appreciate the extent to which English and British constitutional development was a dynamic process. If so he need not have been ashamed for he was in distinguished company. Charles Stuart, king of England, Thomas Wentworth, earl of Strafford, and Edward Hyde, earl of Clarendon, had all made the same mistake. They all had been broken by the same constitution that soon would break Thomas Hutchinson and the empire that he served.

---

[24] Others recognized what Hutchinson missed. Perhaps potentially the most influential was William Pitt. "The resistance to your [parliament's] arbitrary system of taxation might have been foreseen; it was obvious from the nature of things and of mankind; and above all, from the Whiggish spirit flourishing in that country [North America]. The spirit which now resists your taxation in *America,* is the same which formerly opposed, and with success opposed, loans, benevolences, and ship money in *England;* the same spirit which called all *England on its legs,* and, by the Bill of Rights, vindicated the *English* Constitution; the same spirit which established the great fundamental and essential maxim of your liberties, that no subject of *England* shall be taxed, *but by his own consent.*" Speech of Lord Chatham, Lords Debates of 20 January 1775, 1 *American Archives Fourth Series,* at 1496.

ACKNOWLEDGMENTS

This manuscript was edited during a summer's sojourn at the Huntington Library in San Marino, California. In addition to the debt of gratitude owed to the director and staff of the Huntington for their gracious hospitality, thanks are due for generous advice and assistance to John Catanzariti, associate editor of the papers of Robert Morris, to David H. Murdock, of the history department, Leeds University, and to Derek Hirst and David Thomas Konig, associate professors of history, Washington University, Saint Louis. At New York University three persons were very helpful in the work of preparing the manuscript for publication. They were Alan Kaufmann, Martha Webb, and William E. Nelson. Finally, there is Dean Gerald Crane. It was he who called my attention to the great work of Franklin Pierce on these, the briefs of the American Revolution.

Vanderbilt Hall   *JOHN PHILLIP REID*
Washington Square

SHORT TITLE LIST

[Adams,] "Dissertation on Canon and Feudal Law"
[John Adams,] "A Dissertation on the Canon and the Feudal Law,"
reprinted in [Thomas Hollis,] *The True Sentiments of America: Contained
in a Collection of Letters From the House of Representatives of the Province of
Massachusetts Bay to Several Persons of High Rank in this Kingdom* 111–43
(1768).

Adams, "Novanglus"
John Adams, "Novanglus," reprinted in *The American Colonial Crisis:
The Daniel Leonard—John Adams Letters to the Press 1774–1775* (Bernard
Mason, ed. 1972).

Adams, *Works*
*The Works of John Adams; Second President of the United States: with, a Life
of the Author. Volume Two* (Charles Francis Adams, ed. 1851).

Adams, *Writings*
The Writings of Samuel Adams. Volumes Two & Three (Harry Alonzo
Cushing, ed. 1906–07).

[Allen,] "To the Governor"
[John Allen,] "To his Excellency the Governor of the Province of the Massachusetts-Bay," printed as part of [John Allen,] *The American Alarm, or
the Bostonian Plea, For the Rights and Liberties of the People. Humbly Addressed to the King and Council, and to the Constitutional Sons of Liberty in
America* (1773).

American Archives Fourth Series
*American Archives Fourth Series. Containing a Documentary History of the
English Colonies in North America From the King's Message to Parliament, of*

March 7, 1774, to the Declaration of Independence by the United States. Volume I (Peter Force, ed. 1837).

Anon., *Case of Great Britain*

[Gervase Parker Bushe or George B. Butler,] *Case of Great Britain and America, Addressed to the King, and Both Houses of Parliament* (3rd ed. 1769).

Anon., *Free and Candid Remarks*

Anonymous, *Free and Candid Remarks On a late Celebrated Oration; With some few Occasional Thoughts On the late Commotions in America* (1765).

Anon., *Four Letters*

Anonymous, *Four Letters on Interesting Subjects* (1776).

Anon., *Good Humour*

Anonymous, *Good Humour: or A Way with the Colonies. Wherein is occasionally enquired into Mr. P[it]t's Claim to Popularity; And the Principles of Virtuous Liberty, As taught in the School of Mr. Wilkes, and other Peripatetics* (1766).

Anon., *Knowledge of the Laws*

Anonymous, *An Introduction to the Knowledge of the Laws and Constitution of England* (1764).

[Bancroft,] *Remarks*

[Edward Bancroft,] *Remarks on the Review of the Controversy Between Great Britain and her Colonies: In which the Errors of its Author are exposed, and the Claims of the Colonies vindicated, Upon the Evidence of Historical Facts and authentic Records* (1769).

Blackstone, *Commentaries*

William Blackstone, *Commentaries on the Laws of England: Book the Second* (1766).

Boston Declaration

The Votes and Proceedings of the Freeholders and Other Inhabitants of the Town of Boston, In Town Meeting assembled, According to Law [1772].

Brown, *Joseph Hawley*

E. Francis Brown, *Joseph Hawley: Colonial Radical* (1931).

Carroll, "First Citizen"

Charles Carroll, "First Citizen," reprinted in *Maryland and the Empire, 1773: The Antilon—First Citizen Letters* (Peter S. Onuf, ed. 1974).

Cary, *Warren*

John Cary, *Joseph Warren Physician, Politician, Patriot* (1961).

Christie and Labaree, *Empire*

Ian R. Christie & Benjamin W. Labaree, *Empire or Independence 1760–1776: A British-American Dialogue on the Coming of the American Revolution* (1977).

Coke's Reports

The Seventh Part of the Reports of Sir Edward Coke Kt. Chief Justice of the Common Pleas (1738).

Commons Debates 1621
    Commons Debates 1621 [seven volumes] (Wallace Notestein, Frances Helen Relf, & Hartley Simpson, ed. 1935).
Commons Debates 1628
    Commons Debates 1628 [five volumes] (Robert C. Johnson, Mary Frear Keeler, Maija Cole, & William B. Bidwell, ed. 1977–78).
Cushing, "Letter"
    Letter from Thomas Cushing to Arthur Lee (n.d.), September 1773, printed in 4 (Fourth Series) *Collections of the Massachusetts Historical Society* 360 (1858).
Diary and Autobiography
    Diary and Autobiography of John Adams. Volume Three (L. H. Butterfield, ed. 1961).
Dulany, "Antilon"
    Daniel Dulany, "Antilon," reprinted in *Maryland and the Empire, 1773: The Antilon—First Citizen Letters* (Peter S. Onuf, ed. 1974).
Dummer, *Defence of the Charters*
    Jer[emiah] Dummer, *A Defence of the New-England Charters* (1745).
Evening-Post
    Boston Evening-Post
Franklin, *Writings*
    The Writings of Benjamin Franklin: Volume Six (Albert Henry Smyth, ed. 1906).
Gage, *Papers*
    Papers of Thomas Gage (ms., Clements Library, Ann Arbor, Michigan).
Gazette & Post-Boy
    The Massachusetts Gazette and Boston Post-Boy and the Advertiser.
Gordon, *Revolution*
    William Gordon, *The History of the Rise, Progress, and Establishment of the Independence of the United States of America. Volume One* (3rd. American ed. 1801).
Gorges, *A Briefe Narration*
    Ferdinando Gorges, *A Briefe Narration of the Originall Undertakings of the Advancement of Plantations Into the Parts of America. Especially Shewing the beginning, progress and continuance of that of New-England* (1658), reprinted in *Sir Ferdinando Gorges and His Province of Maine*, 18 *Publications of the Prince Society* 1–81 (1890).
Gorges, *Description of New-England*
    Ferdinando Gorges, *A Briefe Narration of the Originall Undertakings of the Advancement of Plantations into the parts of America. Especially Shewing the beginning, progress and continuance of New-England* (1658), reprinted in 6 (Third Series) *Collections of the Massachusetts Historical Society* 44–140 (1837).

[Gray,] *Right of the Legislature*
   [John Gray,] *The Right of the British Legislature to Tax the American Colonies Vindicated; and the Means of Asserting that Right Proposed* (2d ed. 1775).
Grotius, *Rights of War*
   H[ugo] Grotius, *Of the Rights of War and Peace, In Three Volumes; In which are explain'd The Law and Claims of Nature and Nations, and the Principal Points that relate either to Publick Government, or the Conduct of Private Life. Volume Two* (1715).
Hooker, *Ecclesiastical Politie*
   Richard Hooker, *Of the Laws of Ecclesiastical Politie Eight Bookes* [1611].
Hosmer, *Hutchinson*
   James Kendall Hosmer, *The Life of Thomas Hutchinson, Royal Governor of the Province of Massachusetts Bay* (1896).
[Hutchinson,] "Additions"
   [Thomas Hutchinson,] "Additions to Thomas Hutchinson's 'History of Massachusetts Bay,' " 59 *Proceedings of the American Antiquarian Society* 11–74 (Catherine Barton Mayo, ed. 1949).
[Hutchinson,] *Collection of Papers*
   [Thomas Hutchinson,] *A Collection of Original Papers Relative to the History of the Colony of Massachusetts-Bay* (1769).
Hutchinson, "Dialogue"
   Thomas Hutchinson, "A Dialogue Between an American and a European Englishman," 9 *Perspectives in American History* 369–410 (1975).
Hutchinson, *Letters*
   Copy of Letters Sent to Great-Britain, by his Excellency Thomas Hutchinson, The Hon. Andrew Oliver, and Several Other Persons, Born and Educated Among Us (1773).
Hutchinson, *Massachusetts Bay*
   Thomas Hutchinson, *The History of the Colony and Province of Massachusetts Bay* [three volumes] (Lawrence Shaw Mayo, ed. 1936).
[Hutchinson,] *Strictures Upon the Declaration*
   [Thomas Hutchinson,] *Strictures Upon the Declaration of the Congress at Philadelphia; In a Letter to a Noble Lord, &c.* (1776).
"In Our Contracted Sphere"
   John Phillip Reid, "In Our Contracted Sphere: The Constitutional Contract, the Stamp Act Crisis, and the Coming of the American Revolution," 76 *Columbia Law Review* 21–47 (1976).
Journal of the House
   Journal of the Honorable House of Representatives of His Majesty's Province of the Massachusetts-Bay in New England, Begun and held at Harvard-College in Cambridge, in the County of Middlesex, on Wednesday the Twenty-seventh Day of May, Annoque Domini, 1772 (1772 [*sic*]).
Journal of the House of Commons
   Journal of the House of Commons. From November the 8th 1547, In the First

Year of the Reign of King Edward the Sixth, to March the 2d 1628, In the Fourth Year of the Reign of King Charles the First (reprinting of 1803).

[Knox,] *Claim of the Colonies*
  [William Knox,] *The Claim of the Colonies to an Exemption from Internal Taxes Imposed By Authority of Parliament, Examined: In a Letter from a Gentleman in London, to his Friend in America* (1765).

[Knox,] *Controversy*
  [*William Knox,*] *The Controversy Between Great Britain and her Colonies Reviewed* (1769).

[Knox,] *Letter to a Member*
  [William Knox,] *A Letter to a Member of Parliament, Wherein the Power of the British Legislature, And the Case of the Colonists, Are briefly and impartially considered* (1765).

Lee, *Answer*
  Arthur Lee, *Answer to Considerations on Certain Political Transactions of the Province of South Carolina* (1774), reprinted in *The Nature of Colony Constitutions: Two Pamphlets on the Wilkes Fund Controversy in South Carolina by Sir Egerton Leigh and Arthur Lee* 131–205 (Jack P. Greene, ed. 1970).

Lee, *Arthur Lee*
  Richard Henry Lee, *Life of Arthur Lee, LL.D. Volume One* (1829).

Leigh, *Considerations*
  Sir Egerton Leigh, *Considerations on Certain Political Transactions of the Province of South Carolina* (1774), reprinted in *The Nature of the Colony Constitutions: Two Pamphlets on the Wilkes Fund Controversy in South Carolina by Sir Egerton Leigh and Arthur Lee* 63–123 (Jack P. Greene, ed. 1970).

Leonard, "Massachusettencis"
  Daniel Leonard, "Massachusettencis Letters," reprinted in *The American Colonial Crisis: The Daniel Leonard—John Adams Letters to the Press 1774–1775* (Bernard Mason, ed. 1972).

Locke, *Two Treatises*
  John Locke, *Two Treatises of Government* (1772).

Lounsbury, *British Fishery*
  Ralph Greenlee Lounsbury, *The British Fishery at Newfoundland 1634–1763* (1934).

[Mather,] *America's Appeal*
  [Moses Mather,] *America's Appeal to an Impartial World. Wherein the Rights of the Americans, as Men, British Subjects, and as Colonists; the Equity of the Demand, and the Manner in which it is made upon them by Great-Britain are stated and considered. And the Opposition made by the Colonies to Acts of Parliament, their resorting to Arms in their necessary Defence, against the Military Armaments, employed to enforce them, Vindicated* (1775).

McIlwain, "Transfer of the Charter"
  Charles H. McIlwain, "The Transfer of the Charter to New England,

and its Significance in American Constitutional History," 63 *Proceedings Massachusetts Historical Society* 53–64 (1929–30).

Moore, *Cases*
Sir Francis Moore, *Cases Collect & Report per S[ir] Francis Moore Chevalier, Serjeant Del Ley* (2d edition, 1675).

Morison, "Remarks"
Samuel Eliot Morison, "Remarks," 63 *Proceedings Massachusetts Historical Society* 64–65 (1929–1930).

Neal, *History of New England*
Daniel Neal, *The History of New-England Containing an Impartial Account of the Civil and Ecclesiastical Affairs of the Country To the Year of our Lord, 1700* (1720).

Neal, *History (Second Edition)*
Daniel Neal, *The History of New-England, Containing an Impartial Account of the Civil and Ecclesiastical Affairs of the Country, to the Year of our Lord, 1700* (2d ed., 1747).

[Nicholas,] *Proceedings of 1620–21*
[Edward Nicholas,] *Proceedings and Debates of the House of Commons, in 1620 and 1621* (1766).

[Otis], *Rights*
[James Otis,] *The Rights of the British Colonies Asserted and Proven* (1764).

Papers of John Adams
Papers of John Adams: Volume One September 1755—October 1773 (Robert J. Taylor, Mary-Jo Kline, and Gregg L. Lint, eds. 1977).

[Phelps,] *Rights of the Colonies*
[Richard Phelps,] *The Rights of the Colonies, And the Extent of the Legislative Authority of Great-Britain, Briefly Stated and Considered* (1769).

Pownall, *Administration*
Thomas Pownall, *The Administration of the Colonies. Wherein their Rights and Constitution are Discussed and Stated* (4th ed., 1768).

[Prescott,] *Calm Consideration*
[Benjamin Prescott,] *A Free and Calm Consideration of the unhappy Misunderstandings and Debates, which have of late Years Arisen, and yet Subsist, Between the Parliament of Great-Britain, and these American Colonies. Contained in Eight Letters* (1774).

Pufendorf, *Law of Nature*
[Samuel] Pufendorf, *Of the Law of Nature and Nations* (Basil Kennet, translator, 3rd ed., 1717).

[Ramsay,] *Historical Essay*
[Allan Ramsay], *An Historical Essay on the English Constitution: Or, An impartial Inquiry into the Elective Power of the People, from the first Establishment of the Saxons in this Kingdom. Wherein The Right of Parliament, to Tax our distant Provinces, is Explained, and justified, upon such constitutional Principles as will afford an equal Security to the Colonists, as to their Brethren at Home* (1771).

Revolution Documents
  Documents of the American Revolution [volumes four, five and six] (*1973–1974*).
Stevens's Facsimiles
  B. F. Stevens's Facisimiles of Manuscripts in European Archives Relating to America 1773–1783 with Descriptions, Editorial Notes, Collations, References and Translations (1895).
Thorpe, *Charters*
  Francis Newton Thorpe, *The Federal and State Constitutions Colonial Charters, and Other Organic Laws of the States, Territories, and Colonies now or heretofore forming the United States of America. Volume Three* (1909).
Vattel, *Law of Nations*
  M. de Vattel, *The Law of Nations; or Principles of the Law of Nations* (1760).
"Warren Correspondence"
  "Correspondence Between John Adams and Mercy Warren Relating to Her 'History of the American Revolution,'" 4 (Fifth series) *Collections of the Massachusetts Historical Society* 321–491 (1878).

INDEX

69, 77, 96, 128-29, 149; and
limits on crown taxing powers,
36, 49, 60, 68, 69, 93*n*, 116
Mansfield, William Murray, 1st
Earl of, 95 and *n*, 152
Mary II, queen of England:
statutes of, 95, 135-36 and *n;*
proclamation of by parliament, 98 and *n*, 123; colonial
oaths of allegiance to, 139-40
Maryland charter, 58*n*
Massachusetts Bay Colony: civil
disturbances in, 15, 28, 32-33,
84, 85, 86-87, 114, 137, 139;
government of, 18, 38-39,
60-61; and petitions for redress of grievances, 34, 86;
constitutional rights and privileges of, 37-40; appeals from
courts of law in, 64; powers
of *vs.* powers vested in
crown, 64, 73; and supreme
authority of parliament, 66-
71, 101, 142; patent for land
in, 78-79; history of, 78-79,
90, 97-101; town meet-
ings in, 84, 148, 153-54; as
feudatory holding of crown,
95; and acts of trade, 97, 98;
and elevation of William and
Mary to throne of England,
124-25; compact of with
Charles I, 139
—charters of, 15, 30, 58*n*, 60,
79; and legislative power,
18-19, 18*n*, 38-39, 38*n*, 39*n*,
60-62, 67*n*, 68-69, 92; and
reservation of power to parliament, 18, 60-61; and constitutional rights and privileges, 19, 37-40, 37*n*, 41,
62 and *n*, 63, 69-70, 71, 73,
116-17, 160; and supreme authority of parliament, 35,
60-63, 68, 92; provisions of,
37-40, 101, 152; and ap-
pointment of governor, 39;
and taxation, 40, 93-94,
116-17; and laws not repugnant to laws of England, 62,
92, 95-96, 99-100; and acts
of parliament concerning,
99-100; and feudal law, 101,
120-21
—Council of, 18-19, 38-39 and
n; and constitutional debates
of 1773, xi, 5, 6, 14, 27-32,
113-14, 146-47, 157; on cause
of colonial discontent, 32-33;
text of answer to Hutchinson,
32-44; on supreme authority
of parliament, 34-35, 44, 77,
114, 146-47; and doctrine of
consent, 36*n;* reasons for
rejoinder of, 113; rejoinder
of and independence from
crown, 114; authorship of rejoinder of, 114; text of rejoinder of, 114-17
—General Assembly, 62, 154;
and constitutional debates of
1773, 26-27 and *n;* law-
making power of *vs.* parliamentary supremacy, 39,
66-67, 70, 98-101, 138-39,
140-41; and dispute with
Charles II's commissioners,
64-65 and *n*, 97; and taxation,

Virginia (*continued*)

—General Assembly of: and
consent to revenue act, 49-50,
59-60 and *n;* assent of Charles
II to act of, 96

Virginia companies: and James
I, 56, 79; grantees of charter
of, 106 and *n*

Wales: and legislative authority
of parliament, 94, 95

War: crown disposal of territories as spoils of, 88, 129
and *n,* 151

Warren, Dr. Joseph: and authorship of Boston Declaration, 46

Webster, Daniel: on constitutional debates of 1773, 8

Whigs, American: and Boston
Declaration, 2, 46; and
natural law, 2, 20 and *n,* 30
and *n,* 42-43, 42*n,* 50*n,* 86,
86-87*n;* and parliamentary
supremacy, 4, 11, 12, 30, 38*n,*
75-76, 78*n,* 159-60, 163 and *n;*
constitutional principles of, 7,
8-9, 13-14, 41*n,* 72*n,* 162,
163*n;* and emigration theory

of rights, 8-9, 8*n,* 63-64,
64-71; and 17th-century English constitution, 29, 30,
35-36*n,* 163*n;* and constitutional debates of 1773, 29-30,
145-46, 155-56, 158-59 and *n,*
158*n;* and doctrine of consent,
31, 36-37*n,* 82-83; and doctrine of legal resistance, 35
and *n;* and history as authority
for philosophy of, 50-53, 50*n,*
60-63, 64-67, 67-68*n,* 123,
137-42, 137*n;* and
17th-century English whig
philosophy, 115 and *n,*
123-24, 142*n*

William I, king of England: government of and feudal tenure,
149

William III, king of England:
statutes of, 36, 95, 135-36 and
n; proclaimed by parliament,
98 and *n,* 123; and Mas-
sachusetts Bay Colony charter, 99; colonial oaths of allegiance to, 139-40; coronation oath and parliamentary
jurisdiction in the colonies,
140